Presidential Assassinations: The History of Abraham Lincoln, James Garfield, William McKinley, and John F. Kennedy

By Charles River Editors

T. Dart Walker's drawing of Leon Czolgosz shooting President McKinley

About Charles River Editors

Charles River Editors is a boutique digital publishing company, specializing in bringing history back to life with educational and engaging books on a wide range of topics. Keep up to date with our new and free offerings with this 5 second sign up on our weekly mailing list, and visit Our Kindle Author Page to see other recently published Kindle titles.

We make these books for you and always want to know our readers' opinions, so we encourage you to leave reviews and look forward to publishing new and exciting titles each week.

Introduction

The Assassination of Abraham Lincoln (April 14, 1865)

THE ASSASSINATION OF PRESIDENT LINCOLN.
AT FORD'S THEATRE WASHINGTON D.C. APRIL 14TH 1865.

Until April 14, 1865, John Wilkes Booth was one of the most famous actors of his time, and President Abraham Lincoln had even watched him perform. But his most significant performance at a theater did not take place on the stage. That night, Booth became one of history's most infamous assassins when he assassinated President Lincoln at Ford's Theatre in Washington, D.C.

Booth was a member of the prominent 19th century Booth theatrical family from Maryland and, by the 1860s, was a well-known actor. But he was also a Confederate sympathizer who dabbled in espionage, and he was increasingly outraged at the Lincoln Administration. Although Robert E. Lee's Army of Northern Virginia had surrendered days earlier, Booth believed the war was not yet over because Confederate General Joseph E. Johnston's army was still fighting the Union Army, so he and his group of conspirators plotted to kill Lincoln and other top officials in a bid to decapitate the federal government and help the South.

Perhaps not surprisingly, the actor's flair for the dramatic came at a cost to the plot. It took almost no time for the shocked public and the federal government to begin unraveling Booth's conspiracy, which had mostly faltered from the beginning. Following the shooting, America's most famous manhunt commenced, which itself became the stuff of legends. After the shooting, during which it is believed he broke his leg, Booth fled south on horseback, with authorities hot on his tail. 12 days later, while he was at a farm in rural northern Virginia, Booth was tracked down and shot by Boston Corbett, a Union soldier who acted against orders. Eight others were tried for their alleged involvement in the plot and convicted, and four were hanged shortly thereafter as a result of some of the nation's most famous trials.

The Assassination of James Garfield (1881)

"This is not murder. It is a political necessity. It will make my friend Arthur president, and save the republic. … I leave my justification to God and the American people." – Charles Guiteau

In 1880, Civil War veteran James Garfield was running as a Republican for president, and one of his supporters was a man named Charles Guiteau, who wrote and circulated a speech called "Garfield vs. Hancock" that aimed to rally support for the Republican candidate. Though few knew it, Guiteau's family had already deemed him insane and attempted to keep him committed in an asylum, only to have him manage an escape from confinement.

Garfield went on to narrowly edge Winfield Scott Hancock in the election, and Guiteau, harboring delusions of grandeur, believed he had helped tip the scales in Garfield's favor. As such, he believed that he was entitled to a post in Garfield's nascent administration, perhaps even an ambassadorship, and he continued to rack up debts while operating under the assumption that he would soon have the government salary to pay them back. However, despite lobbying around Republican headquarters in New York City and even approaching Cabinet members, no post was forthcoming for the troubled man. Eventually, in May 1881, Secretary of State James Blaine told him to never show up again.

Enraged by the perceived slight, Guiteau bought a revolver and plotted to kill the president. He got his chance on July 2, 1881 at a railroad station, shooting Garfield in the back twice and bragging to the authorities, "I am a Stalwart of the Stalwarts...Arthur is president now!" In reality, Garfield would live for nearly 3 more months, and the poor standards of medical care in the 1880s would end up being responsible for the fact he did not survive wounds that he would've survived at the end of the 19th century. Indeed, Guiteau would cite medical malpractice at trial, stating, "I deny the killing, if your honor please. We admit the shooting."

Those kinds of statements and his generally odd behavior helped ensure Guiteau's lawyers would claim he was insane, one of the first high profile attempts to use that as a defense against a crime. However, that never had much chance of succeeding, and claims of insanity were heartily rejected by prosecutors. George Corkhill, a D.C. district attorney and member of the prosecuting team, insisted, He's no more insane than I am. There's nothing of the mad about Guiteau: he's a cool, calculating blackguard, a polished ruffian, who has gradually prepared himself to pose in this way before the world. He was a deadbeat, pure and simple. Finally, he got tired of the monotony of deadbeating. He wanted excitement of some other kind and notoriety... and he got it."

Throughout his trial, which was all but a foregone conclusion, Guiteau kept up the bizarre antics, including singing in the court, passing notes back and forth with members of the crowd watching the trial, and even openly planning his own 1884 presidential campaign. Of course, those plans were all for naught, because after he was convicted in January 1882, Guiteau was hanged on June 30 of that year. To the end, Guiteau acted oddly, including dancing his way up to the scaffold and reciting a poem he had written as his last words before he met his fate at the gallows.

Garfield was the 2nd president to be assassinated after

Abraham Lincoln, and today he is often remembered as one of the presidents to die in office after being elected every 20 years starting with William Henry Harrison's 1840 election through John F. Kennedy's 1960 election.

The Assassination of William McKinley (1901)

A picture of McKinley speaking in Buffalo the day before he was shot

"It was in my heart, there was no escape for me. I could not have conquered it had my life been at stake. There were thousands of people in town on Tuesday. I heard it was President's Day. All those people seemed bowing to the great ruler. I made up my mind to kill that ruler." – Leon Czolgosz

In September 1901, the city of Buffalo was full of celebration. The Pan-American Exposition was ongoing, and it brought notable figures to northern New York, including President William McKinley, who had been reelected less than a year earlier. But also in Buffalo was Leon Czolgosz, a young man who had turned to anarchy years earlier after losing his job, Embracing his philosophy wholeheartedly, Czolgosz believed it was his mission to take down a powerful leader he considered oppressive, and McKinley's attendance gave him the chance.

President James Garfield had been assassinated just 20 years earlier, but McKinley didn't worry about presidential security or his own safety, and that was the case in Buffalo. McKinley's insistence on greeting the public and shaking hands allowed Czolgosz to walk up to him on September 6, 1901 at a public reception in the Temple of Music on the expo grounds and shoot him point blank, with one bullet grazing the president and another lodging in his abdomen. In the aftermath of the shooting, as Czolgosz was beaten and seized by the crowd, he uttered, "I done my duty." For his part, McKinley said, "He didn't know, poor fellow, what he was doing. He couldn't have known."

Despite being president, McKinley's medical services were shoddy, and given the still primitive medical standards of the early 20th century, gunshots to the abdomen often brought death. One of the best known aspects of the assassination is that Thomas Edison's x-ray machine was on hand and may have been used to try to locate the bullet that doctors couldn't find, but for reasons that remain unknown, the x-ray machine was not used.

Nevertheless, McKinley seemed to improve over the next few days, and people became optimistic he would be all right. As H. Wayne Morgan, one of McKinley's biographers, noted, "His hearty constitution, everyone said, would see him through. The doctors seemed hopeful, even confident ... It is difficult to understand the cheer with which they viewed their patient. He was nearly sixty years old, overweight, and the wound itself had not been thoroughly cleaned or traced. Precautions against infections, admittedly difficult in 1901, were negligently handled." Ultimately, McKinley's wounds became gangrenous a week after he was shot, and after he took a turn for the worse, he died on the morning of September 14, nearly 8 days after he was shot.

McKinley was the 3rd president to be assassinated, and today he is often remembered as one of the presidents to die in office after being elected every 20 years after William Henry Harrison's 1840 election through John F.

Kennedy's 1960 election. However, the most notable consequence of the assassination is who it brought to power. Ironically, New York Governor Theodore Roosevelt's political enemies hoped to rid the state of their progressive governor by elevating him to national prominence. At the Republican National Convention in Philadelphia, the New York machine leaders decided to promote Roosevelt for the vice presidency, and in so doing, remove him from New York. At the time, the vice president was notoriously insignificant in national politics, so the political machinists thought that making Roosevelt the vice president would turn him into a nobody.

Initially, they encountered a problem when McKinley's campaign chief, Mark Hanna, did not think Roosevelt would make a good addition to the Republican ticket. In time, however, they managed to convince Hanna and most other delegates at the National Convention that Roosevelt was the perfect addition to the GOP ticket. Roosevelt was initially unsure of the position; while many thought it would end his political career, Roosevelt wasn't even sure that was a bad thing. Perhaps it was time to return to the countryside, anyway. As a result, after some convincing, Roosevelt accepted the nomination as Vice President alongside President McKinley, and the pair won the election of 1900, making Roosevelt the Vice President in March 1901.

The Assassination of John F. Kennedy (November 22, 1963)

The motorcade seconds before the assassination

In the annals of American history, few moments have been so thoroughly seared into the nation's conscience that Americans can remember exactly where and when they heard about an earth-shattering event. In the 20th century, there was Pearl Harbor and the assassination of President John F. Kennedy.

November 22, 1963 started as a typical Friday, and many Americans were unaware that President Kennedy was even heading to Dallas, Texas. John and Jackie arrived in Dallas in the morning, with Texas Governor John Connally alongside them and Vice President Lyndon B.

Johnson due to arrive later to meet them there. The Kennedys and the Connallys intended to participate in public events later in the day, and Jackie and John were welcomely surprised by the warm reception they received. A public parade was hosted for the President and First Lady that afternoon, and the First Couple rode with the Connallys in an open motorcade en route to a speech Kennedy would deliver later. As they waved to the people lining the streets, around 12:30 p.m. Central Standard Time, Governor Connally's wife turned around to the first couple and said, "Mr. President, you can't say Dallas doesn't love you."

   Moments later, the most controversial assassination in American history took place as a series of shots were fired at the motorcade. The indelible images provided by the Zapruder film of Kennedy being hit in the throat and head, followed by Jackie crawling over the backseat toward the trunk are now instantly recognizable. Within minutes, the news of the shooting began to spread from Dallas across the nation, and everyone's worst fears were confirmed when the President was declared dead about half an hour after the shooting.

   In the wake of the shooting, Lee Harvey Oswald was arrested, proclaimed his innocence, and was then murdered himself by Jack Ruby two days later. The day after that, the President was given a state funeral and procession. The unbelievable chain of events that took place in those 72 hours understandably left the nation shell-shocked.

Despite countless official and unofficial investigations, the assassination is just as mysterious and confusing as ever, and conspiracy theories continue to run rampant nearly 50 years after the assassination. Was Lee Harvey Oswald a patsy? Was he a lone gunman? Was the assassination ordered by the mob?

Presidential Assassinations: The History of the Killing of Abraham Lincoln, James Garfield, William McKinley, and John F. Kennedy chronicles the tumultuous chain of events that led to each president's death. Along with pictures and a bibliography, you'll learn about the assassinations of each president like never before.

Presidential Assassinations: The History of the Killing of Abraham Lincoln, James Garfield, William McKinley, and John F. Kennedy

About Charles River Editors

Introduction

The Lincoln Assassination

  Chapter 1: Plotting Against the President

    The Original Plan

    Attempting the Kidnap

  Chapter 2: From Kidnap to Murder

    The Capture of Richmond

    Reconfiguring the Plot

  Chapter 3: April 14-15, 1865

    The Attack on Secretary of State Seward

    The Assassination of Lincoln

    The Death of Lincoln

  Chapter 4: The Manhunt for Booth

    Booth's and Herold's Escape

    The Capture of Atzerodt and Powell

    Other Arrests

  Chapter 5: Trying the Conspirators

    Military or Civilian Trials?

    The Trials

    Hangings and Imprisonment

  Chapter 6: The Aftermath and Legacy of the Lincoln

Assassination

Lincoln's Funeral

The Garfield Assassination

Chapter 1: A Great Annoyance and Disgrace to His Family

Chapter 2: Determined to Have Revenge

Chapter 3: News of the Horrible Affair Flew

Chapter 4: The Greatness of Their Loss

Chapter 5: Boasting of His Crime

Chapter 6: Grave Responsibility

Chapter 7: An Excuse for Crime

The McKinley Assassination

Chapter 1: The Scene of the Assassination

Chapter 2: The Blackest Friday

Chapter 3: Doctors Were at the President's Side

Chapter 4: Improvement in His Condition

Chapter 5: No Explanation of the Deed

Chapter 6: An Anarchist!

Chapter 7: Guilty

Chapter 8: Wiped from the World

The Kennedy Assassination

Chapter 1: Before Dallas

A Camelot Sized Mirage

The Election of 1960

A Rough Start

Civil Rights Movement

Midterm Elections

Reelection Prospects

Planning a Trip to Texas

Chapter 2: November 21, 1963

Chapter 3: The Assassination of John F. Kennedy

Chapter 4: Chaos in Dallas

Chapter 5: A State Funeral

Chapter 6: Initial Investigations

Chapter 7: Conspiracies

Chapter 8: Legacy

Lincoln and Kennedy

Remembering November 22, 1963

Online Resources

Bibliography

Free Books by Charles River Editors

Discounted Books by Charles River Editors

The Lincoln Assassination

Chapter 1: Plotting Against the President

The presidential box at Ford's Theatre

In November 1863, the Union's fortunes seemed to be on the rise. The victories at Gettysburg and Vicksburg months earlier in July were decisive turning points that would lead to the South's demise. That month Lincoln would travel to Gettysburg to deliver his immortal address, but he also attended a play, *The Marble Heart*, from his box at the newly opened Ford's Theatre in Washington D.C. The lead role was played by one of the country's most famous actors, John Wilkes Booth.

The Booth Brothers acting in Shakespeare's *Caesar*. John Wilkes is on the far left.

At the time, all the public knew about Booth was that he was a dashing actor, well-versed in Shakespeare, and a man so handsome that he constantly received fan mail from women he made swoon. But the man whose favorite Shakespeare role was Brutus had a far more secret side in his life. Booth was a strong Southern sympathizer, even attending the hanging of John Brown after the raid at Harpers Ferry in 1859, and he was an ardent opponent of abolition. On one tour in St. Louis, Booth was actually detained for "treasonous" remarks after he had vocally expressed his desire for Lincoln and the government to go to hell. His partisanship during the war became so bitter that older brother Edwin, who stayed loyal to the Union and wouldn't perform in the South, often avoided confrontation with him.

Booth had a notoriously high sense of self, but he had mostly proved incompetent at anything outside of acting. Booth earned a reputation for having a flair for the dramatic as an actor, and the Southern sympathizer fancied himself a Confederate spy during the early years of the war, at one point using his fame and position as an actor to help smuggle goods into the South past the ongoing blockade. Still, there were plenty of Southerners who had the same resentment of the North and engaged in Confederate activities on a much higher level, and despite Booth's ardent pro-Southern views, he continued to be welcomed and lauded in the North.

It was not until the Election of 1864 that Booth began plotting a daring move. After Vicksburg and Gettysburg had left the Confederacy's hopes of an outright victory in the war looking highly unlikely, the South held out hope that Lincoln would lose his reelection and be replaced by a Democrat who would end the war and negotiate peace with the Confederates. When Lincoln won reelection, the South's fate looked even direr. Booth had not been a soldier during the war, which frustrated him, and his hatred of Lincoln and the North now convinced him to strike a blow.

The Original Plan

Today Booth's assassination of Lincoln is often the only part of the plot that Americans remember, but in November 1864, Booth's plan did not involve murder.

When Lincoln brought General Ulysses S. Grant east and put him in charge of all armies, Grant, William Tecumseh Sherman (now in charge out west) and the Lincoln Administration changed their military policies to one that resembled total warfare. The North's great advantages in manpower and resources would now be more heavily relied upon to defeat the South.

One of the most important changes was that the Union stopped exchanging prisoners of war, a move clearly designed to ensure that the Confederacy would be harder pressed to fill its armies. Originally President Lincoln had opposed such exchanges, believing that giving wartime rights to the Confederacy implicitly acknowledged their independence, but they had been generally welcomed by both sides from almost the beginning of the war. Captives were exchanged and traded throughout the conflict's first few years. Exchanges were often not equal, but were dependent on the rank of the soldiers being exchanged. For example, a captured general was exchanged for 46 privates. One major was worth eight privates while a colonel was worth 15. The varying ranks of the soldiers, with privates at the bottom and generals at the top, allowed for different proportions of exchanges.

Ending the exchange eventually led to atrocities at prison camps like Andersonville and Camp Douglas in Illinois, but it had the desired effect of starving the South of able soldiers. Booth was particularly outraged by this, which many on both sides considered barbaric and contrary to the rules of warfare. In fact, generals on both sides still continued the exchange without informing their superiors.

Out of this termination of prisoner exchanges came Booth's original plan. The North might not be willing to exchange soldiers, but Booth was sure they'd exchange for the President. Thus, Booth began gathering conspirators for a plot to kidnap President Lincoln and use *him* as a negotiating token to get back Confederate troops. Booth figured the President would be worth a great number of soldiers, which would give the rebels a potentially huge and much needed influx of men. A month before Lincoln's reelection, Booth took a trip to Montreal, which was a hotbed for Confederate espionage at the time, and he spent 10 days there. Historians are still unsure what exactly Booth did while there, but many have since speculated that he discussed kidnap plans with better connected members of the Confederate Secret Service and networks of spies.

Kidnap was still the plan when Lincoln's second inauguration took place on March 4, 1865. Despite his hatred of Lincoln, Booth attended the President's second inauguration in Washington. Along with a crowd of over 50,000 spectators, Booth watched as the President took the oath and now delivered his famous second inaugural address on the steps of the unfinished U.S. Capitol Building. Alongside Booth in the audience were several of his eventual co-conspirators: Samuel Arnold, George Atzerodt, David Herold, Michael O'Laughlen, Lewis Powell and John Surratt. All of the conspirators were either from or lived in the Washington, D.C. area or in Maryland, and all were opposed to President Lincoln and were fervent supporters of Confederate secession. With the exception of George Atzerodt, who was born in Germany, all of the co-conspirators were Americans.

In the same month as the President's inauguration, Booth assembled this group of conspirators came together to discuss politics and the ongoing Civil War, as well as the kidnapping plot. Their most regular meeting place, and their most notorious, was the boarding house of Mary Surratt, a Southern sympathizer who would later be alleged of facilitating Confederate espionage. Her son John was an active conspirator with Booth, and people staying at the boarding house would later tell military tribunals that Mary met with him as well.

1890 picture of Surratt's Boarding House

On March 15, the group met at Gautier's Restaurant at 252 Pennsylvania Avenue in Washington, just blocks from the White House. There, they discussed a plan to kidnap the President of the United States, send him to the Confederate capitol in Richmond, and hold him ransom until the Union released Confederate troops. Initially, the most realistic option for capturing the President would be to do so while he was in transit. This ensured that his security detail would be more limited than usual, and his travels were likely to be carried out in less densely populated places, ensuring minimal public awareness of the event. This would allow the group to scurry the President away to Richmond, where he could be held for ransom.

Attempting the Kidnap

Two days later, on March 17, St. Patrick's Day, Booth learned that the President was going to head north to attend a play called *Still Waters Run Deep* at Campbell Military Hospital, located in the northern outskirts of Washington. Because Booth was a member of the nation's acting elite, he was privy to private information about public dignitaries, including the President, attending plays in the D.C. area, the very thing that made his plot possible the following month.

Booth informed his fellow conspirators, and they all agreed to go forward with the plan. Because the President's destination was known and his route could be reasonably assumed, the opportunity presented itself as the perfect one. The conspirators thus assembled along the President's route, hoping to intercept him along his way to the evening matinee. The sun was setting on Washington, providing cover to the conspirators in the darkened streets.

The conspirators were waiting for a man who would never show. To Booth's great dismay, the President had changed his mind and no longer planned to see *Still Waters Run Deep.* Instead, Lincoln attended a ceremony

at National Hotel for the 140th Indiana Regiment, which
was presenting its governor with a captured battle flag.
Ironically, Booth was living at that very hotel at the time.

Chapter 2: From Kidnap to Murder

The Capture of Richmond

With the passing of March, the Civil War had seen
critical developments. General Grant and the Army of the
Potomac had been laying siege to Robert E. Lee's Army
of Northern Virginia at Petersburg since June 1864,
gradually stretching Lee's lines and inching their way
toward the Confederacy's main railroad hub, which was
only miles away from Richmond itself.

Lee's siege lines at Petersburg were finally broken on
April 1 at the Battle of Five Forks, which is best
remembered for General George Pickett enjoying a cod
bake lunch while his men were being defeated. Historians
have attributed it to unusual environmental acoustics that
prevented Pickett and his staff from hearing the battle
despite their close proximity, not that it mattered to the
Confederates at the time. And that would have been
Pickett's most famous role in the Civil War if not for the
charge named after him on the final day of the Battle of
Gettysburg.

When the siege lines were broken at Petersburg, that city
fell the following day, as Lee began a week long retreat

that famously ended with his surrender at Appomattox Court House. On April 3, the Confederate capitol of Richmond fell to Union troops, and days later President Lincoln himself entered the city and even sat at the desk in the Confederate Executive Mansion where Confederate President Jefferson Davis had led the South for nearly the entire war. This was also a significant development for Booth's plot though, because Richmond had been the destination after the conspirators kidnapped Lincoln. Now, to Booth's horror, the President was in Richmond of his own accord. With the city under Union control, where could they bring the President?

Developments in prisoner exchanges had also prompted more fundamental questions among the conspirators. In early 1865, General Grant agreed to resume prisoner exchanges on a man-for-man basis, believing the war was nearing its end. His intended to negotiate exchanges until all prisoners from both sides were released. Capturing the President had been intended to serve as a negotiating piece in discussions over prisoner exchanges, which General Grant had earlier stopped. With exchanges resumed, what purpose was there in kidnapping Lincoln?

The Old Soldiers Home, where the conspirators planned to kidnap Lincoln

Reconfiguring the Plot

Booth's original plan now lay in shambles, and all of the conspirators were now compelled to reconsider their purpose. Richmond was no longer a viable place to take the President, there was no obvious reason to take the President at all since prisoner exchanges were back in action, and the war was clearly nearing its end. Kidnapping the President would do nothing to bring the Confederacy back into existence or save slavery in the South.

Booth didn't care, continuing to hold out hope of a Confederate victory. To understand Booth's rationale, it is important to remember that General Joseph E. Johnston, who Lee famously replaced at the head of the Army of Northern Virginia, still had a sizable army opposing General Sherman's army near the Carolinas. Although Appomattox is generally regarded as the end of the Civil War, there were still tens of thousands of Confederates in the field throughout April 1865, and Jefferson Davis himself was still holding out hope while fleeing from Richmond. Thus, Booth still intended to help the Confederacy somehow.

Two days after Appomattox, Lincoln gave a speech at the White House in which he expressed his desire to give former slaves the right to vote, a policy that would come to fruition through the 13th, 14th, and 15th Amendments. Naturally, such a policy infuriated Southerners, and Booth was so enraged by the speech that he was later alleged to have claimed, "Now, by God, I'll put him through. That is the last speech he will ever give."

On April 11, the other conspirators still believed the conspiracy was about kidnapping Lincoln, and there was dissension in the ranks. Samuel Arnold and Michael O'Laughlen informed Booth of their intention to not participate in any kidnapping of the President. For them, the resumption of the prisoner exchange program and the coming end of the war made holding the President for ransom a moot point. They chose to disassociate themselves of the entire conspiracy.

Everyone else was still on board, but the group as a whole needed to regroup. Kidnapping the President made less sense than it had before, but these conspirators agreed that something still needed to be done. Various plans were thrown around, including John Surratt's thought that blowing up the White House with a bomb would be the easiest and most effective method of dealing with the President. Surratt had connections with Confederate bomb-making experts who he thought could mine the White House and destroy it. This unlikely plot was made even more unlikely when Thomas Harney, the Confederacy's bomb expert who Surratt considered most likely to successfully bomb the White House, was captured by Union forces on April 10.

While Surratt was in Montreal, likely networking with Confederate spies, Booth and the remaining conspirators were still in Washington. Together they devised a more feasible, though also more complicated, plan to assassinate high-ranking members of the federal government. It would take a miracle to save the South, and they figured the chaos that would ensue with a leaderless national government might do the trick. On April 13, Booth and the conspirators met at the Surratt

Boarding House and hatched a plan to assassinate Lincoln, Vice President Andrew Johnson, and Secretary of State William Seward, a sinister plot they thought would throw the federal government into disarray at a critical moment in its history.

Given the manner in which the plot changed, it's not surprising that the conspiracy was still riddled with glaring errors. For whatever reason, the plot overlooked Secretary of War Edwin Stanton, who in many respects asserted the most authority in the wake of Lincoln's assassination before the government began functioning normally again. And Booth pegged conspirator George Atzerodt to be the one to kill Vice President Johnson, even after Atzerodt objected to the murder plots and asked out of the conspiracy.

Now that the conspirators had their new plot, they still needed to figure out when they would carry it out. As fate would have it, they didn't have long to wait.

Atzerodt

Chapter 3: April 14-15, 1865

One of the most decisive days in American history began for Booth at midnight, who found himself wide awake laying in bed. In his diary entry for the day, Booth wrote, "Our cause being almost lost, something decisive and great must be done". But when he woke up, Booth was unaware that the plot would be carried out that night.

Lincoln, on the other hand, slept more than usual. The day was Good Friday, and it was one of the first days in many years that Lincoln was relatively stress free. Though he still had plenty of work to do, its urgency paled in comparison to the decisions he had had to make during the war. After the capture of Richmond and Appomattox, Lincoln now focused more on how to reconstruct the nation than winning the war. At around

8:00 a.m., the President and his son ate breakfast together at a leisurely pace.

Later that morning, he met with many dignitaries to discuss logistics about Reconstruction. He met with Speaker of the House Schuyler Colfax, General Grant, the Governor of Maryland and Senator Creswell, also of Maryland. At 11:00 a.m., the President held a special Cabinet Meeting with General Grant in attendance. Grant relayed intimate details of the surrender at Appomatox to the Cabinet, and the Cabinet discussed what to do about Confederate leaders now that the war had been won. Lincoln hoped they would simply flee the country. Either way, he thought good news was to come, telling his Cabinet that he had a dream the previous night in which he was flying away in some sort of vessel at an indescribable speed. He had had this dream before major victories in the war, and thought it was a harbinger of positive developments. General Grant, on the other hand, reminded the President that many of the other times the President reported the dream, the Union had lost battles. The President remarked to his Cabinet that, either way, something big was going to happen. Cabinet officials would later note how unusually happy Lincoln was, with Secretary of the Treasury Hugh McCulloch noting, "I never saw Mr. Lincoln so cheerful and happy."

At the end of the meeting, around 2:00 p.m., President

Lincoln asked both General Grant and Secretary of War Stanton if they would like to join the Lincoln's at Ford's Theatre later that evening. As it turned out, Stanton and Grant were hearing about Lincoln's plan for the night after Booth had already learned it. Both declined the offer, but Lincoln had already conveyed his plan to bring Grant that night to the people at Ford's Theatre. When Booth stopped by the theater at noon to pick up mail from his permanent mailbox, owner John Ford's brother casually mentioned the president would be attending *Our American Cousin* that night, a play Booth knew so well that he later timed his shooting of Lincoln in conjunction with the play's funniest line, which Booth figured would help him because it would draw the loudest laughs.

Now Booth was set on killing Lincoln during the play. That afternoon he arranged with Mary Surratt to have a package delivered to her tavern in Maryland. Booth had previously stored guns and ammunition at the tavern, and he asked Surratt to inform one of her tenants to have those ready for him to pick up there. It would be this meeting that doomed Mary Surratt to her fate of becoming the first woman executed by the federal government.

After some paperwork, Lincoln and Mary Todd went for a carriage ride throughout the capital, enjoying the fresh air and relaxing environment for nearly two hours. When they returned to the White House, they asked Illinois

Governor Richard Oglesby if he wanted to join them at Ford's Theater. He, too, declined. Ultimately, Major Henry Rathbone and his fiancée Clara Harris, the daughter of a New York Senator, accepted the invitation and became Lincoln's guests in the presidential box that night.

Rathbone

At 7:00 p.m., Booth and the other conspirators convened to put the plot in motion. Lewis Powell, a rough and tumble veteran who had suffered a battle wound at Gettysburg, was to break into Secretary of State Seward's home, accompanied by David Herold. There, they were to assassinate the Secretary, who was still weak and recovering from wounds he had suffered in a carriage accident. The same evening, George Atzerodt was to head to the Kirkwood Hotel, where Vice President Johnson was living, and assassinate him as well. All of the attacks were to take place simultaneously around 10:00 p.m., and the conspirators agreed on an escape spot in Maryland to meet up after the attacks.

Between 8:00 and 8:30, the Lincoln's left the White House, and arrived at Ford's Theater shortly thereafter. They were late for the play, which began at 8:00 p.m. A special box on the second story balcony was decorated for the President's arrival, and the Lincolns, Major Rathbone, and Clara Harris settled into their spots and enjoyed the show. They were initially guarded by a policeman, John Frederick Parker, but for reasons that are still unclear, Parker left his post during the middle of the play and headed to a tavern with Lincoln's coachman.

When Booth had heard Grant was attending the play, either he or O'Laughlen followed Grant, who was boarding a train to head to Philadelphia, not Ford's Theatre. It's believed that O'Laughlen attempted to attack Grant that night, but Grant and his wife were too heavily protected by staff onboard the train, and the car they were riding in was locked.

The Attack on Secretary of State Seward

Seward

Powell

Often lost in the aftermath of Lincoln's assassination is Lewis Powell's unbelievable attack on Secretary of State Seward. In fact, Powell's attack on Seward was the first attack of the night. On the other side of Washington D.C., Seward was in his home still convalescing from a carriage accident on April 5 that left him with a concussion, a broken jaw and a broken arm. One of the most famous aspects of the attack was that Seward was wearing a neck brace, but in fact doctors had put together a splint to help his jaw repair.

Shortly after 10:00 p.m., Powell, dressed as a pharmacist and carrying a revolver and a Bowie knife, knocked on the door of Seward's home. The butler answered the knock, at which point Powell told the butler he needed to speak with the Secretary personally, to instruct him how to take his medication.

The butler let him in, but as soon as he entered, Seward's son Frederick stopped him. Not recognizing Powell, Frederick told him Seward was sleeping and could not be awoken, but just as he said that, Seward's daughter opened a door and told them the Secretary was awake. Powell now knew his location, pointed a gun at Frederick's head, and fired. Luckily, the gun misfired, and after the burly Civil War veteran bludgeoned Frederick with the gun and knocked him out cold, the gun was broken.

Powell wouldn't be able to shoot Seward, but he still had the Bowie knife. After knocking out Frederick, Powell rushed wildly into Seward's room and began stabbing at Seward's neck and face, knocking him out of the bed and onto the floor. When Seward's daughter screamed, it awoke Seward's other son, Augustus. Together with the sergeant on detail there, the two began wrestling with Powell, who still managed to stab them and Seward's daughter as they tried to fight him off.

After stabbing those three, Powell fled the scene, only to

run directly into a messenger with a telegram at the door. Powell stabbed him in the back and exited the house, only to find that co-conspirator David Herold had abandoned him and fled when he heard the commotion coming from the house. Powell left the scene on horseback, but he had no clue how to get to the meeting spot in Maryland and instead began hiding out in Washington D.C.

Seward had been badly wounded, but not fatally. The jaw splint had deflected Powell's stabs away from the jugular vein, and Seward would go on to recover.

The Assassination of Lincoln

While Secretary of State Seward was under attack, Ford's Theater was in still in the middle of *Our American Cousin*. Booth had suggested the attacks take place around 10:00, but he entered the theater just before 10:30. Because he was a well-known and widely admired actor, no one thought twice about letting him in. Admissions simply assumed he was interested in viewing the play. Moreover, nobody would have thought twice about granting Booth access to Lincoln's presidential box, even if the guard had been in his proper position.

Just at 10:30, the play was at Act III, Scene II, and the actor Harry Hawk was alone on the stage when a gunshot echoed across the theater. The President's bodyguard was absent, having ambled across the street to the nearby tavern. Without having to worry about the bodyguard, Booth was able to penetrate the double-doors of the President's box easily, and he barricaded the first door behind him with a stick so that the President could not escape.

  Booth knew *Our American Cousin* by heart, having seen it numerous times. He waited between the doors until Hawk uttered the funniest line of the play. When the audience erupted in laughter, Booth made his shot, striking the President in the back of the head. The President slumped forward, and Mary immediately began screaming while grabbing the back of his shirt.

The pistol Booth used.

  At this time, Mary Lincoln, Rathbone and Clara Harris were still the only ones who were aware the president had been shot. As Lincoln slumped forward, Rathbone lunged at Booth to try to stop him, but Booth pulled out his knife and stabbed Rathbone twice before jumping out of the balcony down to the stage, about 12 feet below. It is widely believed that Booth suffered a broken left leg during the jump when his foot got entangled in the flag decorating the box. Always the showman, Booth got up to his feet, crossed the stage, and reportedly yelled "Sic semper tyrannis", which was Virginia's state motto and Latin for "thus always to tyrants."

The crowd was still in a state of confusion while Booth made his last appearance on stage, but Mary and Rathbone were yelling out "catch that man," at which point the audience realized that the excitement was not part of the play. Some members ran towards Booth, but no one was able to capture him, and Booth was able to hop onto the horse he had waiting for him outside and escape.

Having likely suffered a broken leg, Booth knew his part of the assassination plot hadn't gone directly according to plan, but he had no way of knowing just how poorly the rest of it had gone. Herold and Powell had been separated, with Powell failing to kill Seward, but even that was more of a success than George Atzerodt's attack on Vice President Andrew Johnson. This is because that attack never took place. Atzerodt, who Booth insisted on tabbing for the attack on Johnson despite his objections to murder, had lost his nerve while drinking at the Kirkwood's hotel bar. Instead, the drunk Atzerodt roamed the city's streets that night, but only after he had asked the bartender about Johnson, which obviously drew suspicion when news of the attacks on Lincoln and Seward spread. The next day, police searched the room Atzerodt had booked and found a revolver and Bowie knife.

The Death of Lincoln

After the shooting, a doctor in the audience named Charles Leale rushed towards the President's box, only to find that Booth had sealed the door. Together with another doctor in the audience, Charles Sabin Taft, the two men assessed the President's state. He had no pulse, and at first Leale believed him to be dead. The two doctors unbuttoned the President's shirt to try to find the bullet hole before discovering the bullet had entered the back of the President's head. Leale removed blood clots from the hole, which helped Lincoln start to breathe better.

Regardless, both doctors immediately believed the President's wound was mortal and that he would not recover. The two men, together with another Doctor Albert King, consulted on the state of the President. They agreed it was best for him to die in comfort, and not in the box in the theater. However, a bumpy carriage ride back to the White House, which would almost certainly draw a crowd, was not a reasonable option.

The three doctors and some soldiers in the audience carried the President's body across the street, where Henry Safford told them the President could stay in his residence. A bed was prepared, though the President was too tall and needed to lay on it diagonally. At this point, the Petersen House became the de facto headquarters for the federal government and the manhunt for Booth, who had already been immediately identified as the assassin by the time he exited the theater.

The Petersen House

Presidential physicians, including the Surgeon General and Lincoln's personal doctor, arrived to assess the state of the President. They all agreed that the President would not survive.

At this point, news of the shooting began to spread, with

Secretary of the Navy Gideon Welles and Secretary of War Stanton rushing over to the Petersen House to all but take control of the federal government. Understandably, Lincoln's wife Mary was a complete wreck, sobbing so loudly that Stanton at one point ordered people to remove her from the room. Indeed, when they arrived, the situation was as grave as they were told, and doctors thought the President would survive for only a few more hours. Physicians, including Canada's first African-American doctor, Anderson Ruffin Abbott, continued to work on the President throughout the night, but the hemorrhaging of his brain could not be stopped.

  The following morning, at 7:22 a.m., President Lincoln died, surrounded by Senator Charles Sumner, Generals Henry Halleck, Richard Oglesby and Montgomery Meigs, and Secretary of War Stanton. Mary was not present; she was too distressed throughout the night to see the President. As Lincoln took his last breath, legend has it Stanton famously said, "Now he belongs to the ages." (Other historians speculate he said, "Now he belongs to the angels.")

Stanton

Chapter 4: The Manhunt for Booth

Herold

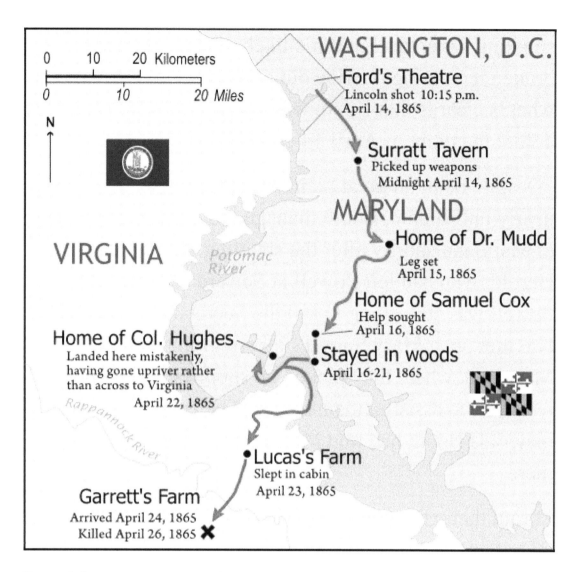

Booth's and Herold's Escape

Given the lack of technology and the delays caused by the shock of Lincoln's assassination, the manhunt for Booth and the unraveling of the conspiracy occurred extremely quickly. Much of the conspiracy was done in by bumbling errors made by the men who didn't escape, while the manhunt for Booth was greatly aided by his broken leg. It is widely believed that Booth suffered a broken leg jumping from the presidential box after shooting Lincoln. If not, it's likely that he suffered a broken leg during the ride out of Washington. Either way, what is clear is that Booth was hampered by a broken leg before the night of April 14 ended.

Despite being in great pain that made horseback riding nearly unbearable, Booth managed to escape, as planned, to Maryland shortly after the shooting. So did David Herold, who had left Powell at Seward's house while Powell was still trying to kill the Secretary of State. The two met up at Mary Surratt's tavern in Surrattville, Maryland, where they picked up supplies, including a revolver, to assist in their escape. These included the materials Booth had told Mrs. Surratt to ensure would be there.

From there, the two continued southward to the home of a Dr. Samuel Mudd, where they arrived at about 4:00 a.m. on April 15. The doctor set Booth's fractured leg in a cast, and he furnished Booth with crutches. Controversy still exists today over the extent of Mudd's involvement in Booth's escape, and whether he was an unwitting plan or had foreknowledge of Booth's conspiracy. Although it is known that Mudd and Booth knew each other dating back to 1864, Mudd proclaimed his innocence until his death, but Atzerodt later told federal investigators that Mudd knew about the plot ahead of time. Either way, Mudd waited until Sunday, April 16, to get word to authorities that Booth and Herold had been there, which ultimately made investigators suspicious.

Within hours of the assassination, Secretary of War Stanton began coordinating the manhunt with authorities. In addition to posting a $100,000 reward for the capture of Booth and his co-conspirators, federal troops had dispersed across Maryland and northern Virginia in search of them, while an investigation of accomplices ensued in Washington.

After spending more than half of April 15 at Dr. Mudd's home, Booth and Herold hid in the swamps and woods of rural Maryland along their escape route to the South. The following day, they made it to the home of a mutual friend, Samuel Cox, in southern Maryland, who helped them contact Thomas Jones. Jones was a Confederate spy who agreed to assist the two in navigating their escape. From there, Jones escorted the two through the woods of southern Maryland from April 16-21, but they did not travel much distance in that time, which would prove crucial because the manhunt was bearing down on them. Booth's injury had made traveling great distances too difficult.

Once the two crossed the Potomac, they crossed the farmland of Virginia, settling down in various farms along the route. By April 24, 10 days after the assassination, the pair made it to Garrett's farm. Incredibly, the family was still unaware of Lincoln's assassination, making it possible for Booth to convince the family that he was an injured Confederate soldier who had trekked through the woods of Virginia for days in search of help.

Unbeknownst to them, federal authorities were closing in on them. The manhunt naturally assumed that Booth would be heading south from Washington D.C., where he would be more likely to find sympathizers and aid in the Southern states. When they found out Mudd had set his leg, it confirmed a southern route.

Still, the federal authorities and soldiers pursuing Booth had no clue where he was on April 25. Lieutenant Edward P. Doherty, who was leading the 16th New York Cavalry, later wrote in his official report that they only "had reliable information that the assassin Booth and his accomplice were somewhere between the Potomac and Rappahannock Rivers." That day, while interrogating men near a ferry spot, the 16th New York Cavalry learned that men matching Booth's and Herold's descriptions had crossed via that very ferry the day before on their way to the house of a Mr. Roland. Moreover, they learned that Booth and Herold had tried to hire someone to take them to Bowling Green, which as it turned out was 12 miles away from Garrett's Farm.

Booth met his fate early on the morning of April 26, when Doherty's unit of about 30 men surrounded Garrett's

Farm and quickly learned from Mr. Garrett that Booth and Herold were in the barn. Doherty explained what happened in his official report:

Sergt. Boston Corbett, Company L, Sixteenth New York Cavalry asked permission to enter the barn alone, which I refused. Booth all this time was very defiant and refused to surrender. At one time he said if we would draw up in line fifty paces off he would come out, adding that he was lame and had only one leg. This, however, I refused. Booth up to this time had denied there was anyone in the barn besides himself. Considerable conversation now took place between myself, Booth, and the detectives. We threatened to burn the barn if he did not surrender; at one time gave him ten minutes to make up his mind. Finally, Booth said, "Oh; Captain, there is a man here who wants to surrender awful bad:" I answered, and I think Mr. Baker did at the same time, "Hand out your arms." Herold replied, "I have none." Baker said, "We know exactly what you have got." Booth replied, "I own all the arms, and intend to use them on you gentlemen."… Almost simultaneous with my taking Herold out of the barn the hay in the rear of the barn was ignited by Mr. Conger, and the barn fired. Sergt. Boston Corbett, Company L, Sixteenth New York Cavalry, shot the assassin Booth, wounding him in the neck. I entered the barn as soon as the shot was fired, dragging Herold with me, and found that Booth had fallen on his back. Messrs. Conger and Baker, with some of my men, entered the barn and took hold of Booth."

The unit had orders not to kill Booth, so the soldiers lit the corners of the barn on fire in order to smoke Booth out. However, when Sergeant Boston Corbett spotted Booth near the back door of the barn holding two guns, he mortally wounded Booth with a shot to the spine. Booth spent the next two hours paralyzed, and shortly before his death, he asked a soldier to hold up his hands. Looking at his hands, Booth uttered his last words, "Useless. Useless."

Although they had intended to take Booth alive, Doherty wrote, "I beg to state that it has afforded my command and myself inexpressible pleasure to be the humble instruments of capturing the foul assassins who caused the death of our beloved President and plunged the nation in mourning." Corbett was actually placed under arrest for disobeying orders, but the charges were dropped at the behest of Secretary of War Stanton himself. Each member of the 16th New York Cavalry collected a share of the reward for Booth's death, receiving over $1,500 each. Over the coming decades, Corbett was so volatile and unstable that he was eventually placed in an insane asylum in the 1880s.

Corbett

The Capture of Atzerodt and Powell

  Amazingly, despite being the only one instantly identified as one of the conspirators, and despite being killed less than two weeks after the assassination, Booth was the last of the main conspirators to be captured. It took federal soldiers 12 days to capture Booth and Herold, but it took far less time for Powell and Atzerodt to literally walk themselves into custody.

  On the night of April 14, while his co-conspirators were carrying out their attacks and fleeing, George Atzerodt was stumbling around. Atzerodt was supposed to assassinate Vice President (now President) Andrew Johnson, but he got so drunk that he spent the nights walking throughout the city. Apparently, he never spent any part of the night in the hotel room he had booked. However, when Atzerodt asked the bartender where Vice President Johnson was sleeping, the curious question would lead authorities straight to him.

The bartender contacted the police, who were now fully engaged in a city-wide manhunt and investigation. The following day, the military police searched Atzerodt's room, finding a revolver and a bank book belonging to Booth. This was sufficient evidence to warrant arresting Atzerodt. On April 20, George Atzerodt was arrested without a fight, in Germantown, Maryland, where he had been staying with his cousin since leaving the hotel.

Meanwhile, Powell unwittingly unraveled the rest of the conspiracy for authorities. After attacking the Secretary of State, Powell exited the home to find that his accomplice, David Herold, had already fled. Powell was now being chased by Seward's family and neighbors, so he fled the scene on horseback, leaving his weapons behind. Powell fled to a cemetery in a Washington suburb, where he discarded remaining evidence and remained for some time. He hid in a tree there for three days, aware that he was being chased, but unsure of the route to the agreed-upon Maryland meeting location.

Obviously Powell knew he could not hide out in public forever, but without having any clue how to get to a safe place in Maryland, the only viable location he could think of was the boarding house of Mary Surratt, where the conspirators had met on so many occasions.

Powell could not have picked a worse time than the evening of April 17 to reappear at Mary Surratt's boarding house. Through a combination of factors, including the information relayed through Surratt's African-American servants, federal authorities tied Surratt's son John to the attempt on Seward, and they came to believe Mary Surratt was somehow involved in the plot. The boarding house's association with Booth had been attested to by witnesses as well.

When authorities entered her home, Mary denied having any involvement in the plot. She also lied about her son's whereabouts and the fact she had helped Booth arrange to pick up a package at her tavern on April 14. On the night of April 17, as authorities were getting ready to charge her for the conspiracy, Powell showed up at her door in disguise, claiming he was there to dig a ditch. Mary claimed not to recognize Powell, but not surprisingly, the authorities did not believe Powell was there to dig a ditch at night. And given how often Powell was at the boarding house, Mary's claim not to recognize him struck the authorities as yet another lie. Both Powell and Surratt were arrested that night.

Other Arrests

Ironically, Mary suffered a far worse fate than her son, despite the fact he was almost certainly more involved in the conspiracy. John Surratt Jr. also proved to be far more difficult to catch. At the time of the assassination, he was in Elmira, New York, nowhere near Washington, D.C. However, interrogations of arrested conspirators led authorities to believe he was involved in the plot. By then, he had fled to Montreal, Canada, where he was protected by Roman Catholic priests.

Surratt didn't just seek safety north of the border. Eventually, he fled overseas to England, where he assumed the name John Watson. From there, he became nomadic, moving around Europe and North Africa, while federal authorities maintained a warrant for his arrest. He even served briefly in the army of the Papal States, but in November 1866, more than a year after the murder, an old American friend traveling through Italy recognized Surratt and alerted the American Embassy. He was arrested on November 7, and sent to an Italian prison, but managed to escape, and fled to Alexandria, Egypt, where he was again arrested by U.S. authorities on November 23. He was sent home via ship to Washington, D.C., where he was imprisoned in early 1867.

In addition to the conspirators most directly involved in the assassination of the President and the attempted assassinations of Secretary of State Seward and Vice President Johnson, dozens more were arrested on related charges, though many were later released.

Two of the original conspirators, Samuel Arnold and Michael O'Laughlen, were both arrested, despite backing out of the plot when it turned into an assassination scheme. Arnold was arrested in Fortress Monroe, Virginia, after authorities found correspondence between him and Booth that pertained to a plot against the government. Arnold proved especially critical to the government, as he had backed out of the plot and was willing to give extensive information to authorities. This information led them to another former conspirator, Michael O'Laughlen. He voluntarily surrendered himself in Baltimore.

In addition to Mary Surratt and Powell, several other important arrests were made on April 17. Among them was Edman Spangler, a Ford's Theatre employee who held Booth's horse in the back of the theater so that the assassin could make an easy escape. The owner of the theater himself, John Ford, was arrested as a suspicious character. A boarder at Surratt's home, and Booth's own brother were also incarcerated. Many others who were tangentially connected to the supply chain of the assassination and escape were arrested, including the stable owner who sold Booth a horse, Dr. Mudd, Samuel

Cox and Thomas Jones, who had helped Herold and Booth escape through Maryland and Virginia.

Chapter 5: Trying the Conspirators

Military or Civilian Trials?

The killing of Booth and the apprehension of the conspiracy's main players was remarkably successful, but the means of trying the conspirators, and who to try for what, was an open question among military officials. The events were intimately connected to the Civil War, but they were also carried out by civilians independent of any military body. And though the authorities tried desperately to see if there was a connection between the assassination and the upper reaches of the Confederate government (including the recently captured Jefferson Davis), the inability to find hard evidence connecting Booth to actual Confederates ensured the way to try the people caught was heavily debated. For example, Secretary of War Stanton supported a military tribunal to be followed by executions, but former Attorney General Lincoln Bates favored a civilian trial, believing a military tribunal was unconstitutional given the circumstances.

In the aftermath of Lincoln's death, members of the government worried that a military tribunal and execution of Lincoln's assassins would turn *them* into martyrs. In the long run, it didn't. While the South was not traumatized at all by Lincoln's passing, they were not eager to laud the plot against the federal government. To many, even in the South, Booth's and the conspirators' actions were dishonorable. The South recognized that it had lost, and Booth's actions were viewed as a foolish attempt to save the Confederacy.

To resolve the issue, President Johnson asked sitting Attorney General James Speed to prepare a reasoned brief defending his position on the issue. Speed reasoned that, because the President was assassinated before the complete cessation of the Confederate rebellion, the issue was properly handled by the war department, as it was an act of war against the United States. A military tribunal was thus decided. On May 1, 1865, President Johnson ordered a nine-person military tribunal be set up to try to the alleged assassins. The members of the commission were: Generals David Hunter, August Kautz, Albion Howe, James Ekin, David Clendenin, Lewis Wallace, Robert Foster, T.M. Harris and Colonel C.H. Tomkins.

Holding military tribunals greatly affected the ability of the conspirators to defend themselves. The rules of the commission stipulated that a simple majority vote would lead to a conviction, while a vote of two-thirds or more meant the death penalty. All conspirators were offered legal counsel, if they wanted it, but the tribunal did not assure them basic trial rights afforded by the Constitution either. In particular, evidence like hearsay that would never be admissible in regular trial courts was allowed in the military tribunal.

The Trials

Ultimately, only eight conspirators were charged and tried by the military tribunal: Samuel Arnold, George Atzerodt, David Herold, Samuel Mudd, Michael O'Laughlen, Lewis Powell, Edman Spangler and Mary Surratt. The trials began on May 9, 1865, and lasted for seven weeks, ending on June 30th, 1865. It was held on the third floor of the Old Arsenal Penitentiary.

Library of Congress

Photograph of the District penitentiary, about 1865, after it had been taken over by the United States Army for use as an arsenal.

The prosecution team charged with trying to convict the eight consisted of General Joseph Holt, John A. Bingham and HL Burnett, lawyers.

Lewis Powell's trial was the most convincing, since the assassin failed to kill his target and was witnessed by many in the Secretary of State's family. Additionally, the circumstances of his arrest added further evidence against him. Authorities had eye-witness reports against Powell, and he left guns and other belongings behind on his escape route. The best his defense attorney could do was to argue that his life not be taken because he was an insane fanatic. Regardless, Powell was found guilty and sentenced to death by hanging.

The evidence against David Herold was just as incriminating. He was, after all, apprehended in the company of Lincoln's assassin, John Wilkes Booth. Worse, Herold was proud of the crime, and bragged about it throughout the proceedings. His attorney had little hope for saving his client's life, and relied on the argument that Herold was a simpleton, too stupid to realize the gravity of his crime, and that his life should therefore be spared. The military tribunal didn't buy the argument and sentenced Herold to death by hanging.

The remaining defendants were not so easily prosecuted. George Atzerodt had not killed anyone, and explicitly said he was not interested in doing the job. Regardless, his hotel room showed correspondence with Booth and he had a gun under his pillow, suggesting he second-guessed his reluctance to kill the Vice President. His defense attorney used his cowardice to try to prevent Atzerodt from receiving the death penalty, noting his client was too cowardly to ever go through with the assassination. However, Atzerodt also took no active steps to stop the murder conspiracy despite his knowledge of it, and he went on the run after April 14 and hid out. The military tribunal eventually decided that he, too, deserved death by hanging.

Mary Surratt

Mary Surratt was the last and most controversial defendant to receive a conviction of death by hanging. Just about everyone believed she facilitated the conspiracy in critical ways, from the use of the boarding house to ensuring Booth could pick up supplies from her tavern, but did she know the intent of the conspiracy or play an active enough role to warrant death? Her culpability was rarely doubted, but she was among the most hotly defended. More witnesses testified on her behalf than any other defendant, and due to the nature of her involvement aiding and abetting the assassins, hers was a more evidence-intensive trial. The government relied on witnesses to attest that she had conspired with the assassins, including being present in meetings held by Booth and the other major conspirators. Meanwhile, her attorneys tried to portray Surratt as a woman loyal to the Union, who would not support killing the President. They also tried to impeach the testimony of the people who testified against her, including neighbors and servants, and knock out their testimony as unreliable. However, all of these defenses were undermined by the fact that, in the moments of her arrest, Powell came to her home with weapons and a clear intent to hide out. And her claim that she did not recognize Powell that night, despite the fact he had frequently met other conspirators in her boarding house, greatly damaged her believability. Although Powell would tell authorities Surratt was completely innocent, Atzerodt told authorities she was more deeply involved in the conspiracy than even authorities believed. Eventually she was thus convicted and sentenced to death by hanging. When President Johnson signed her death warrant, he is said to have remarked she "kept the nest that hatched the egg".

The remaining four defendants did not receive death

sentences. Dr. Samuel Mudd, who set Booth's broken leg, was charged with aiding Booth in his escape. His defense focused on Mudd's being a Union man who treated his slaves well. Others testified against this, arguing that Mudd was indeed a Confederate sympathizer. Even still, authorities could prove no connection to the conspiracy other than the fact Mudd helped an injured Booth in the middle of the night on April 15, not exactly the most damning evidence. Mudd barely escaped the hangman, avoiding the death penalty by one vote, and was instead sentenced to life in prison. His guilt, however, was endlessly doubted, until President Johnson pardoned the doctor on March 8, 1869, in part because he had served ably as a doctor during a yellow fever outbreak at the prison in Fort Jefferson.

Dr. Mudd

Samuel Arnold's and Michael O'Laughlen's trials were very similar to the prior ones pertaining to aiding and abetting the assassins. Because they did not directly participate in the attacks, their trials focused on their loyalty to the Union and reluctance to kill. Those defenses spared them the death penalty, but not life in prison. Like Mudd, Arnold was pardoned in 1869, but O'Laughlen died of yellow fever in 1867 while at Fort Jefferson.

Finally, Edmund Spangler, who had watched Booth's horse while he shot the President, was given the lightest sentence of the eight, at six years in prison. The evidence against him was highly questionable, as many were uncertain that he knew the purpose of watching Booth's horse was to kill the President. Spangler allegedly thought the horse was poorly tamed, and simply needed someone to keep an eye on it. Because of this, he was only sentenced to six years in prison. He served a shorter sentence, however, when President Johnson also pardoned him in 1869.

Hangings and Imprisonment

Because the eight had been sentenced by military tribunal, the Commander-in-Chief needed to give his ultimate seal of approval before action could be taken. When the trial ended on June 3[h], the Commission forwarded its report to President Johnson, who signed the death warrants. It marked the first time a woman had been sentenced the death penalty by the U.S. government, a step that alarmed even some of the judges of the tribunal, who asked Johnson to commute Surratt's death sentence.

Mary Surratt's lawyers hurried together a review to be done in lower courts, but President Johnson quashed the review, saying that a military tribunal sentence could not be appealed in civilian courts.

On July 7, 1865, Union General Winfield Scott Hancock brought the four convicted assassins to the Old Arsenal Penitentiary in Washington, D.C., around noon. At 1:30, the trap underneath the hanging four was removed, and Mary Surratt, George Atzerodt, Lewis Powell and David Herold fell to their deaths.

The death warrants are read before the hangings.

The execution of Mary Surratt, Powell, Herold, and Atzerodt

In August 1867, John Surratt was brought back to the United States from Egypt, where he was tried in a civilian court. The jury was hung on his case, and he was thus not guilty. He was released from prison and began a speaking tour, detailing the conspiracy across the nation. Despite almost certainly being more involved in the conspiracy than his mother, Surratt lived out the rest of his life a free man.

Apart from Michael O'Laughlen, who died in prison, the remaining conspirators were released by President Johnson in an eleventh hour pardon before he left office in early 1869. The President's pardons outraged the North. Not only did he pardon the assassins, but he also pardoned high-ranking members of the Confederacy, and offered excessive clemency.

Chapter 6: The Aftermath and Legacy of the Lincoln Assassination

Lincoln's Funeral

Abraham Lincoln was not the first president to die in office, nor the first president to be shot at (an assassin tried to kill President Andrew Jackson nearly 30 years earlier). But he was the first American President to be assassinated.

After the President's death, his body was moved to the White House, where he lay in state in a temporary coffin. There, the President's body was prepared for burial. A public viewing took place from 9:30 a.m. until 5:30 p.m. on April 18th, which was followed by a private viewing for two hours afterwards. A short, private service was held in the Green Room.

Funeral procession in Washington

From there, the Lincoln Funeral in Washington, D.C., began on April 19 at 2:00 p.m., when the President's body left the White House for the last time, and travelled down Pennsylvania Avenue to the Capitol Rotunda. Six gray horses carried the President's coffin. Despite an enormous crowd, the procession was nearly silent, except for a dim drumming and the sounds of the horses' hooves. Once the procession reached the Capitol, the President's body was escorted up the very steps on which he was inaugurated less than two months earlier. The coffin was brought into the Capitol Rotunda, where his body remained alone overnight.

The following day, the Rotunda was opened for a public viewing of the President. At around 7:00 a.m., the public began flowing through the Capitol, with a steady stream coming through consistently until the sun began to set.

On April 21, the President's body finally left Washington, for the beginning of a long train route back to Illinois. The train embarked on a nationwide viewing, which began in nearby Baltimore, Maryland. From there, the train moved on to the following sites: Harrisburg, Pennsylvania; Philadelphia; New York City; Albany, New York; Buffalo; Cleveland; Columbus, Indianapolis; Michigan City, Indiana; Chicago; and, finally, Springfield, Illinois. The President's body lay in state at each location.

Lincoln's funeral was, and still is, widely regarded as the greatest funeral in the history of the United States. Never before, or since, has a single person passed through so many communities: though the President's body only rested in state in the previous communities, the funeral train passed through over 400 towns and cities.

Once in Springfield, the President lay in state a final time before being brought to the Oak Ridge Cemetery for burial. Alongside his son William Wallace Lincoln's body, the two were moved to a receiving vault on May 4th, 1865. The Lincoln Tomb was still under construction, and would not be complete for some years, when Lincoln was relocated.

Being the first American President assassinated, President Lincoln's death shook the nation to its core. After four years of unprecedented trauma, Lincoln had guided the nation through the Civil War, only to become in some ways one of its last victims. On May 23-24, to commemorate the end of the war, regiments of the Union Armies held a Grand Review of the Armies, parading through the streets of Washington D.C. Famous leaders like Generals Sherman and Grant were present, as were the government's top officials, but Lincoln's absence could not help but be felt by everyone.

Still, it's necessary to remember that his untimely death transformed him into a martyr and dramatically altered his legacy in American history. At the time of his death, Lincoln's image transformed overnight. On April 14, Lincoln was a solid, but controversial, President. For much of his presidency, he was under attack from all sides: Democrats considered him a power grabber disregarding the Constitution, Republicans didn't like his policy plans for Reconstruction, many didn't respect the Westerner they considered to be too coarse, and the South despised him. Put simply, Lincoln may have been appreciated among freed blacks in the South and people in the North for leading the nation through the Civil War, but he was not the titanic figure he is today.

However, in the generation after the Civil War, Lincoln became an American deity and one of the most written about men in history. Furthermore, the gravity of his legacy skyrocketed on the morning of April 15. The tragedy and unexpectedness of his death, coupled with its violence, helped turn Lincoln into a martyr, and Lincoln's accomplishments were solidified. Lincoln had ended slavery in the South and ensured that the Union remained undivided. He had also put in place Reconstruction policies that would help lead to sectional reconciliation and the Civil War Amendments, which ended slavery, gave minorities voting rights, and provided equal protection of citizens against the actions of the states. Without question, these accomplishments earned Lincoln a place in the pantheon of American legends.

At the same time, Lincoln had clearly reached the apex of his presidency with the defeat of the Confederacy. With a second term fully ahead of him, there's no telling how mired his legacy would have been by Reconstruction, which pitted Radical Republicans against President Johnson and Democrats. The Republicans wished to subject the South to harsher treatment than Johnson's conciliatory policies, and even though many in the South were allowed to take loyalty oaths, many continued to intimidate, suppress, and kill blacks, remaining "unreconstructed". Eventually, the South was put under martial law and turned into military districts put under the control of the federal army. Reconstruction would not officially end until 1876, and while there's no question that Lincoln would have governed more competently than Andrew Johnson, there's also no question that Reconstruction during his second term would have tarnished his record, and ultimately, his legacy.

Nevertheless, those alternatives remain what ifs, and historians today widely consider Lincoln the country's greatest President. There is equally little question that his assassination helped propel him to that position. With his tragic death, the aura of martyr would not surround Lincoln, and his record might have looked far different if he left office in 1868. The Abraham Lincoln we know today owes its origins to the events of April 14, 1865, and the hands of one man: John Wilkes Booth.

The Garfield Assassination

Chapter 1: A Great Annoyance and Disgrace to His Family

"He was one of the first persons, after the election, to send to General Garfield for an appointment. … He appeared in Washington during General Garfield's visit there, before the inauguration, and construed, or pretended to construe, a promise to see him again into the promise to grant him an appointment as consul at Marseilles. He frequently stated to persons from whom he borrowed money, and to the proprietors of boarding-houses where he owed for his board, that the appointment was promised to him, and he should soon be able to pay his debts. Some persons excused his eccentricities and dishonesty by the thought that he was insane, and his father, before he died, seemed to think that his son's persistent lying and swindling was the result of a diseased brain. But when the peculiarities of his father's religious opinions and eccentric behavior, which were often exceedingly strange, are noted with the fact that his mother died in his infancy, leaving him without maternal care or advice, we can see much in his circumstances and hereditary disposition to account for his crimes. Not enough, however, to lead the public to believe that he was actually insane. He was a great annoyance and disgrace to his family, and none felt the shame more keenly, or denounced the crime more strongly, than did those who lived to hear of his terrible crime." – Russell H. Conwell, *The Life, Speeches, and Public Services of James A. Garfield, Twentieth President of the United States* (1881)

July 2, 1881 began like any other day in post-Civil War America. Independence Day was approaching, and with it a series of parades, political speeches and town picnics. James Garfield, inaugurated as president of the United States just a few months earlier, was looking forward to an enjoyable time that day speaking at his own alma mater, Williams College, and getting away from the heat of Washington for a few days. As it turned out, however, Garfield would never give the speech he had prepared, nor would he ever enjoy any of the festivities planned for the holiday. In fact, he would never make it to catch the 9:30 a.m. train he was scheduled to take before Charles Julius Guiteau stepped in his way and shot him twice.

Pictures of Guiteau

After such a heinous crime takes place, people often claim the accused seemed normal, but no one who knew him would ever say that about Guiteau. He was born in 1841 to a severely mentally ill mother and a father overwhelmed by his wife's behavior. After his mother died in 1848, Guiteau's father turned him over to his older sister Franky to raise while he worked and tried to find another wife. Later, when the elder Guiteau did remarry, his new wife found it difficult to deal with the boy, who could neither speak plainly nor keep still for more than a few seconds at a time.

By the time he was in his mid-20s, Guiteau had found an outlet for his personality in religious fanaticism, which had him traveling the country preaching and writing books primarily concerned with the end times. He was also a moderately successful con-man who typically left each town with a trail of debt behind him. He later told the judge in his trial, "I will tell you how I do it, Judge, and perhaps you can learn if you want to borrow money. … I come right out square with a friend. I do not lie and sneak and do that kind of business, or anything. I say, 'I want to get $25; I want to use a little money;' and the probability is that if he has got the money about him, he will pull the money right out and give it to me. That is the way I get my money. I take it and thank him and go about my business. … If a man has the money, he gives it to me on a sudden impulse, I suppose; and if he has not, that settles it."

When the religious obsession waned or he failed at his most current pursuit, he took on a new passion: politics. Guiteau found fertile ground for his interest during the 1880 Republican primaries by becoming a part of the Stalwart faction, which was determined to see Ulysses

Grant nominated for a third term. Opposing them were the Half-Breeds, a group backing James Blaine of Maine. In the end, neither faction mustered enough votes to win, which resulted in a compromise candidate, James Garfield, being nominated.

Guiteau seemed satisfied when Garfield chose Stalwart Chester Arthur to be his running mate. He often volunteered at the Republican headquarters in New York City. He often asked to be allowed to speak at public functions but was allowed to only once, to a small group of barely franchised African-American voters.

Garfield/Arthur campaign placard. *Currier & Ives*

Arthur

Unfortunately, when Garfield won the general election, Guiteau's diseased mind believed that it was largely due to his speech. He immediately began to write to the president-elect, informing him of his good works and asking for a political appointment, and in the weeks following Garfield's March inauguration, Guiteau became even more demanding, insisting that he deserved a diplomatic post somewhere overseas. After requesting a position in Vienna, Guiteau asked for one in Paris. By the middle of May, Blaine, whom Garfield had made his Secretary of State, had had enough and told Guiteau on the 14th, "Never bother me again about the Paris consulship so long as you live."

Blaine

Despondent, Guiteau focused his rage and disappointment on Garfield, concluding that the only way to make things right was to remove the man he felt he had put in office from the White House. Indeed, he came to believe that he was under divine direction to do so.

By the middle of June, Guiteau had formulated a plan, so he borrowed $15 with which to purchase a .45 caliber snub-nosed revolver. It was later asserted that Guiteau bought that kind of gun because it would look good in a museum following his historic act.

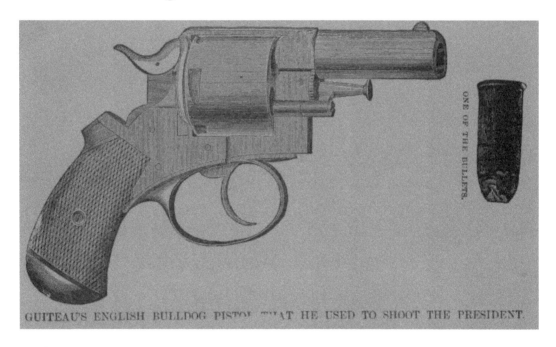

ONE OF THE BULLETS.

GUITEAU'S ENGLISH BULLDOG PISTOL THAT HE USED TO SHOOT THE PRESIDENT.

Guiteau's Pistol. Drawing by James Dabney McCabe

A picture of the pistol, now housed at the Smithsonian

Regardless of whether that's true, he was certainly intent on taking action, and the following day, June 16, he began writing an "Address to the American People," which seemed to have fully set forth his views: "I conceived the idea of removing the president four weeks ago. Not a soul knew of my purpose. I conceived the idea myself and kept it to myself. I read the newspapers carefully, for and against the administration, and gradually the conviction dawned on me that the president's removal was a political necessity, because he proved a traitor to the men that made him, and thereby imperiled the life of the republic. … Ingratitude is the basest of crimes. That the president, under the manipulation of his secretary of state, has been guilty of the basest ingratitude to the stalwarts, admits of no denial. The expressed purpose of the president has been to crush Gen. Grant and Senator Conkling, and thereby open the way for his renomination in 1884. In the president's madness he has wrecked the once grand old Republican Party, and for this he dies. … This is not murder. It is a political necessity. It will make my friend Arthur president, and save the republic. … I leave my justification to God and the American people."

When asked during his trial about his rationale for killing Garfield, Guiteau replied, "I would not have accepted the Paris consulship, if the President had urged it and Mr. Blaine had urged it upon me with the utmost determination, any time after the 1st of June. … I would not have done it, because my mind was fully fixed as to the necessity of the President's removal for the good of the American people. I would not have taken the Paris consulship at any time after the 1st of June. … I would have sent it right back any time after the 1st of June. My whole heart and mind and inspiration was in removing him. … If General Garfield had had the proper respect for [my] letters, things would have been very different today. But what did he do but sell himself, soul and body, to Mr. Blaine. …he did not appreciate the sentiment and kindness of those letters, but put himself into Mr. Blaine's hands, and allowed Mr. Blaine to use the Presidency to crush Grant and Conkling, and the very men that made him."

Chapter 2: Determined to Have Revenge

 "Mortified at his failure to obtain the coveted appointment, and angry beyond expression because of his forcible ejection from the White House, he determined to have revenge. Various schemes suggested themselves to him, according to his own confession, which would bring disgrace and failure upon the administration and shame upon the President, but none would or could satisfy him but the murder of General Garfield. … He believed that if he could wreak his vengeance at such a time he would have the sympathy and support of the President's political enemies. Although they never knew Guiteau or communicated with him, and never said aught to show the slightest sympathy with such a horrible idea, yet he was angry enough to entertain the idea that they would come to his relief, especially as the Vice-President, who would be promoted, was the most intimate supporter and outspoken sympathizer with Senator Conkling. How unfounded and unreasonable were his conclusions was subsequently demonstrated. Arming himself with a heavy revolver, he determined to obtain his revenge by shooting the President. He had a hard task to overcome the remonstrances of his own heart. Again and again he started to do the deed, and crept back a coward before his own conscience." – Russell H. Conwell, *The Life, Speeches, and Public Services of James A. Garfield, Twentieth President of the United States* (1881)

Political cartoons depicting Guiteau in the wake of the shooting

Once Guiteau had made up his mind to kill Garfield and had armed himself, he merely had to find an opportune moment in which to commit the deed. In late June, he actually followed Garfield's carriage from the White House to Blaine's home, but he decided at the last minute not to attempt to kill the president that time. On another occasion, he followed the President to a railway station, thinking that would be the perfect place in which to shoot him, but according to one source, he was deterred by the presence of Garfield's wife. "[T]he affectionate husband lifted his wife from the carriage, and Guiteau saw her thin hands and pale, sweet face, he was defeated again; and, stuffing his revolver in his pocket, said, 'I'll wait till she is better.'" Although he tarried in those instances, Guiteau made careful plans to avoid being carried off and killed by the angry mob that would no doubt form upon Garfield's death, for he believed that if he made it safely to the jail, those who agreed with him politically would no doubt arrange his release.

Then, on June 30, the local newspaper reported that Garfield would be taking the 9:30 train out of the Baltimore and Potomac Station, bound for Williams College in Massachusetts, on July 2. Guiteau arose early that morning, took his new gun, and went down to a secluded river bank near his home, where he practiced his aim until he was sure that he could hit his intended target. After that, Guiteau proceeded to the train station to await his victim.

Baltimore & Potomac Terminal. National Gallery of Art.

Once he reached the station, Guiteau took up his post in the Ladies Sitting Room, which the president would have to pass to reach his own train. A woman named Mrs. White was in charge of the Room that day and described the shooting: "I had noticed this man Guiteau lounging around the ladies' room for a half hour before the arrival of the' President. I did not like his appearance from the first time I saw him. It is my business to see that such characters do not loaf around the ladies' room, and I thought seriously of having him pointed out to our watchman, Mr. Scott, so that he should be made [to] stay in the gentlemen's room. When the President and Secretary Blaine entered he was standing near the entrance door. He wheeled to the left and fired, evidently aiming for the heart. It was a quick shot and struck the President in the left arm. The President did not at first seem to realize that he had been struck, although Secretary Blaine instantly stepped to one side as though dazed at this unexpected movement. The President then partly turned around and the assassin advancing two steps fired the second time — the whole thing being the work of a few moments. The President advanced one step, then fell to the floor. I ran to him at once and raised his head and held it in that position until some gentlemen came, and we remained until his son came from the car where he was seated, with the rest of the Presidential party, awaiting the arrival of his father."

The *Associated Press'* depiction of Guiteau shooting Garfield

According to other witnesses, after shooting Garfield, Guiteau calmly wiped his pistol clean and put it in his pocket. He then turned to leave, having ordered a cab to take him directly to the jail.

Police officer Patrick Kearney may have been the last person to speak to Garfield before he was shot. He recalled, "I thought that that was a peculiar thing, but before I could follow it up closer I saw the President's party driving down Sixth Street to the depot, and I had to go and look after them. They drove to the B Street entrance. Secretary Blaine was with the President, and the two entered the depot together. The President walked up to me, and asked how much time he had before the train left. It was twenty minutes after nine o'clock I saw by looking at my watch, and I told the President that he had ten minutes. Just as he thanked me I heard a pistol shot, and turning, I saw the man that I had been watching previously standing about ten feet away, in the shadow of the main entrance to the waiting-room, levelling his pistol across his arm. He fired a second shot before I could speak to him, and darted between myself and the President and Secretary Blaine into the street. The President reeled and fell just in front of me. As he fell he said something I could not exactly understand, and Secretary Blaine, with a terrified look, pushed towards him, exclaiming, 'My God, he has been murdered! What is the meaning of this?' 'In God's name, man,' I shouted, ' what did you shoot the President for?'"

The Illustrated Newspaper's depiction of Garfield just after being shot

Mr. Parks, who worked at the train station, witnessed the shooting and remembered, "I had been watching for the arrival of the President through the small window between my office and the ladies' waiting room, and saw this man Guiteau, who was a small man, slight in physique, with short pointed beard on his chin. His movements were those of an uneasy, nervous man. At that time there were but few persons present, and nearly all ladies. I was attracted by the report of a pistol. I immediately peered into the ladies' room and saw the assassin, pistol in hand, standing about two feet inside of the entrance door. I saw him advance two paces and fire the second shot. … There was an interval of about four seconds between the first and second shots. Just as soon as the second shot was fired I took in the situation, and ran out of the office for the purpose of securing the assassin. In the meantime Guiteau tried to make his escape by the main door on Sixth Street, but being headed off he turned to make away by the exit of the ladies' room on C Street, when I grappled him by the left hand and the left shoulder, and held him until Officer Kearney and Depot Watchman Scott came to my assistance in a few moments, the former holding him by the right shoulder and the latter securing him by his clothing in the back. He said that this letter which he held in his hand and flourished frantically about his head was going to General [William Tecumseh] Sherman and explained all. When I first laid my hand on him he made desperate efforts to release himself, but upon finding that it was useless he subsided."

In fact, the letter the Guiteau had in his hand, which he apparently dropped as he was being hauled away, read, "I have just shot the President. I shot him several times as I wished him to go as easily as possible. His death was a political necessity. I am a lawyer, theologian, and politician. I am a Stalwart of the Stalwarts. I was with General Grant and the rest of our men, in New
York during the canvass. I am going to the Jail. Please order out your troops, and take possession of the jail at

once." Naturally, when General William Sherman heard about the shooting and the letter, he stated emphatically, "I don't know the writer, never heard of or saw him to my knowledge, and hereby return it to the keeping of the above-named parties as testimony in the case."

As the crowd began to cry out that Guiteau be lynched, Kearney got him out the door and to a nearby police station. All the while, Guiteau was calmly reassuring those around him, "It is all right, it is all right. I am a Stalwart."

Chapter 3: News of the Horrible Affair Flew

"The President's son Harry, scarcely realizing what had happened, for but little blood fell from the wounds, stood ready to fight or die in his father's defense. The scene beggars description. A beautiful summer morn, warm and tranquil as the face of nature in early spring, encouraged the brightest thoughts and happiest feelings in the hearts of the company that was to journey with the President. Now their countenances were black with sorrow. 'President Garfield assassinated!' exclaimed Secretary Hunt. 'Impossible!' …word was sent to Surgeon-General Barnes, Drs. Norris, Lincoln, and Woodward, requiring their immediate presence at the depot. With the messengers trooping over the pavements it was not long before every part of Washington was informed of what had happened, and the fact became generally known.

Then a crowd soon assembled, and in less than ten minutes Sixth Street and B Street were packed with people, and the news of the horrible affair flew from mouth to 'mouth and spread over the city like wildfire. An attempt was made to rush into the building, and cries were raised to lynch the assassin; but a strong force of policemen, summoned by telephone, had arrived promptly on the scene and preserved order. In the meantime the President had been carried to a room up-stairs and the physicians summoned." – J.S. Ogilvie, *History of the Attempted Assassination of James A. Garfield* (1881)

Still lying on the Ladies' Room floor wounded, Garfield's head was cradled in Mrs. White's lap, and she held him gently, crying throughout the ordeal as he began to vomit and go into shock. Reporter James Young managed to get into the room and later wrote, "The first person I saw was Secretary Windom. He was standing alone, as pale as death, and the tears were trickling down his cheeks. Knowing him well I said : 'Mr. Secretary, where is the President, and what does this mean?' He replied, 'There he lies in yonder corner in that group. It is as much of a mystery to me as it is to you.' I moved over about two yards, and there I saw the President lying on a mattress which had been hastily brought from the sleeping apartments of one of the depot employees. There were probably thirty people around him, many of whom were women, who had been waiting for the southern trains. Secretary Blaine had hold of one of the President's hands, and Postmaster-General James was assisting to get him into a sitting posture. His face showed a deathly paleness, and he had a look of surprise, as if caused by pain and despair. He was vomiting and seemed to have no control of himself. His coat and vest had been ripped from him and his trousers loosened. The matter he had vomited had fallen on his shirt below the bosom, which made it seem as if the ball of the assassin had penetrated the intestines."

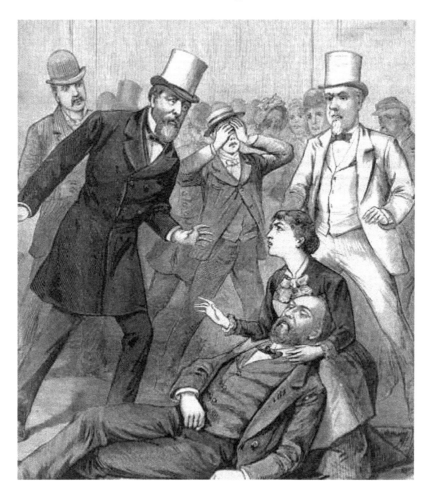

A depiction of Garfield being held by Mrs. White

Tragically, two of Garfield's sons, James and Harry, were also with him that day. Mrs. White remembered, "When I ran to him he was deathly pale, but perfectly conscious. In about two or three minutes he vomited. His son was kneeling beside him at this time. He asked me if I saw who shot his father, and I replied, ' Yes, and he is caught.' He said somebody would have to pay for this. The young man and I thought the President was dying, so pale was he. He tried to raise his head and get his hand on the wound near the thigh, but he was too weak to do so. I noticed Guiteau at the depot either early this week or the latter part of last."

A picture of Garfield's children, with James and Harry standing

Young also observed this scene: "Near him was his son, a lad of sixteen. Poor boy, he was almost beside himself. He wrung his hands and cried in a piteous manner. With him were the son of Colonel Rockwell, and Secretary Hunt, who, in every way natural to human beings, were trying to comfort him."

Of course, the comfort of the family would have to take a backseat to caring for the injured president. Young continued, "In less than ten minutes Secretary Blaine gave orders to have the President removed to the upper floor of the depot, to the officers' room, where there would be plenty of air and a freedom from the mob which was rapidly gathering. Colonel Rockwell and Adjutant-General Corbin soon made a passage way, and the President was borne by a number of the colored porters of the depot to the upper floor. I waited down-stairs, and in about half an hour he was carried down, placed in an ambulance, and under a strong guard of mounted police was driven to the White House. I immediately left the depot and hurriedly went up Pennsylvania Avenue. Although it was not an hour since the shooting took place, I found the avenue crowded with people, some standing in groups, regardless of the broiling hot sun, discussing the event, others hurrying towards the depot, and others pushing and rushing and wending their way no one knows where."

Rockwell

Dr. Smith Townshend, the local District Health Officer, was the first doctor to reach the fallen President. He recalled, "I arrived at the depot four minutes after he was shot, and found him lying upon the floor of the depot, surrounded by an immense gathering. He was then in a fainting condition. From his appearance and the pulsations at the wrist I thought he was dying. I took some of the pillows from under his head that he might rest easier. I prescribed aromatic spirits of ammonia and brandy, which revived him. I ordered the police to get the crowd back, and had the President removed to an upper room. He rallied considerably, and I proceeded to examine his wounds. I found that the last bullet had entered his back about two and a half inches to the right of the vertebrae.

When I placed my finger in the wound some hemorrhage followed. I then administered another dose of the stimulant, which again revived him. In the meantime Drs. Purvis and Bliss arrived. I had, however, previously asked him how he felt and where the most pain was felt, and he answered in his right leg and feet. I asked him the character of his pain, and he said that it was a pricking sensation. Dr. Woodward, of the army, also came in afterwards, and after a consultation we concluded to remove him to the White House. It was then about ten o'clock, and all the members of the Cabinet were present. …after I made the examination of the wounds the President looked up and asked me what I thought of it. I answered that I did not consider it serious. He continued, 'I thank you, doctor, but I am a dead man.'"

Soon, there were 10 other doctors from around the city, and they ordered mattresses pulled out of nearby sleeper cars and put in the back of an express wagon. The President was placed on board and driven carefully back to the White House, where he was placed in his own bed. Townshend continued, "When we arrived at the White House, and just before he was removed from the ambulance, he asked me to call to Major Brock to clear the hall, as there might be another assassin around. Quite a number of the doctors and others went along with the ambulance. When taken from the ambulance he was in a fainting condition, and we revived him with stimulants, and upon consultation we concluded to give a hypodermic injection of morphia and allow him to rest until three o'clock. Afterwards we gave him an injection of atropia and morphia, which brought his pulse up to eighty. At three o'clock, when we had another consultation, we found his pulse 102 and temperature 96, or two and a half below normal. While we were in consultation he became very much nauseated and vomited considerably. Upon examining the wound we found much dulness and tension of the right hypogastric region, restlessness and pain, which indicated internal hemorrhage. We immediately gave him one hypodermic injection of a quarter of a grain of morphia, which relieved him of the pain and quieted him. At half-past four o'clock this afternoon, when I left him, he was in a partially comatose state and unconscious. He was not talking much, but answered some of our questions."

An illustration depicting doctors discussing Garfield's condition.

Some of the doctors who examined him more closely had few encouraging words for him. One said aloud, "He is dying. Look at his eyes; they are becoming fixed."Another one asked, "Why don't we do something?" Needless to say, this did not bolster the president's morale, and it was left to his wife Lucretia, who arrived and lifted his spirits by telling him, "Well, my dear, you are not going to die as I am here to nurse you back to life; so please do not speak again of death."

Lucretia Garfield

On July 5, Blaine's wife wrote to one of their children, "Maggie, nurse, came running into the room crying, 'They have telephoned over to you, Mrs. Blaine, that the President is assassinated.' Emmons flew, for we all remembered, with one accord, that his father was with him. By the time I had reached the door, I saw that it must be true — everybody on the street, and wild. Mrs. Sherman got a carriage and drove over to the White

House. Found the streets in front jammed and the doors closed, but they let us through and in. The President still at the station, so drove thitherward. Met the mounted police clearing the avenue, then the ambulance, turned and followed into that very gateway where, on the 4th of March, we had watched him enter. I stood with Mrs. MacVeagh in the hall, when a dozen men bore him above their heads, stretched on a mattress, and as he saw us and held us with his eye, he kissed his hand to us — I thought I should die: and when they brought him into his chamber and had laid him on the bed, he turned his eyes to me, beckoned, and when I went to him, pulled me down, kissed me again and again and said, 'Whatever happens, I want you to promise to look out for Crete,' — the name he always gives his wife. . . . 'Don't leave me until Crete comes.' I took my old bonnet off and just stayed. … At six, or thereabouts, Mrs. Garfield came, frail, fatigued, desperate, but firm and quiet and full of purpose to save, and I think now there is a possibility of succeeding.

In doing so, Mrs. Blaine soon became a witness to history. She described the events of the following day: "After breakfast I went with your father to the White House, and finding that their arrangements for nursing were all made for the day, I came immediately away. It looks as though Mr. Garfield would live. He is now, six o'clock, still comfortable and has asked for beefsteak.

They will not, of course, let him have it. Mrs. Sherman and Tom were there, who came to let the President and Mrs. Garfield know that yesterday the men of his order made their communion an offering for the President's recovery. Your father has stayed in and read and signed dispatches and received callers, and now W. and your father have gone to the White House to make inquiries and thence to pay their daily visit to V.P. Arthur, who is on Capitol Hill. . . . When I was with the President yesterday, as I was all the forenoon, he looked up at me and said, 'When I am ready to eat, I am going to break into Mrs. Blaine's larder.'"

Chapter 4: The Greatness of Their Loss

"The most skillful physicians of the country including Dr. Bliss, Dr. Agnew, and Dr. Hamilton were called to Washington; Mrs. Garfield was taken by a special train to her husband; and every appliance which human skill has invented, and which could give any relief or hope, was immediately brought into use. The physicians gave some encouragement that the President could possibly recover and for eighty long days and nights the nation eagerly scanned every bulletin from the physicians with almost breathless suspense. The Cabinet officers remained in attendance on the wounded President, some of them laying aside for the time their port-folios to take up the merciful task of watching and nursing at the bedside. As day after day of his sufferings passed, the anxious people felt more and more the greatness of their loss, and as they heard day by day his expressions of Christian resignation and trust their love for him grew strong and pure. The devotion of Mrs. Garfield and the affection of the mother and children became themes for poets and essayists. The purity of character and heroism of the wife were so touching, so sublime, that she became a loved sister or daughter to all the people." – Russell H. Conwell, *The Life, Speeches, and Public Services of James A. Garfield, Twentieth President of the United States* (1881)

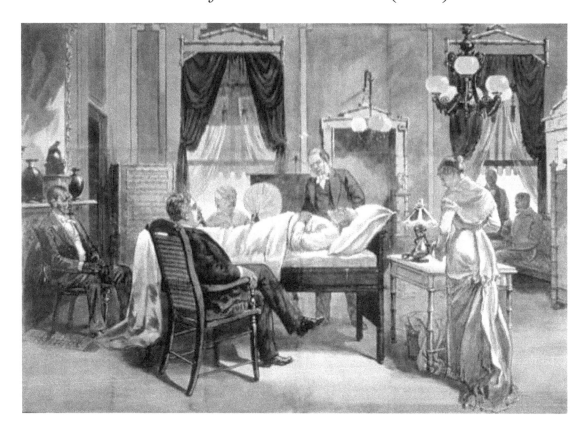

***Harper's Weekly* illustration of Garfield convalescing in bed**

With his family gathered around him, Garfield slept through the first night, disturbed only by periodic bouts of vomiting, and the next morning, he had full bowel and urination function, as well as a normal temperature and strong pulse. With these signs that there was no organ damage, the doctors began to feel more optimistic, and on July 8, Mrs. Blaine could write to her kids, "Everything seems to be going as well with the President as the most loving heart can wish. … No danger now, no anxiety about paralysis, or bullet in the liver, and every prospect of a speedy recovery in all his parts. … I have been to the White House this morning, but saw none but officials. Left your father there in consultation with the doctors. … I suppose you have noticed that the President came here Friday afternoon. … Now it seems this Guiteau followed him to this house, waited to shoot him on his return, but not wanting to hurt Secretary Blaine, had to give it up that time."

As the days went by, it seemed increasingly likely that the president might indeed survive his wounds, and by mid-July, Blaine himself wrote, "Garfield, I think, is surely destined to be much more speedily well and out than is generally thought. I differ from the doctors about the direction of the ball — have never believed that the liver was pierced at all — and think the event will prove that I am right." After another week passed, Mrs. Blaine wrote, "Your father saw the President for six minutes yesterday morning, the first time since that fateful Saturday. They had put him…off day after day, till he would be denied no longer. He looked better than your father expected to see him, though his voice was weak. Mrs. Garfield told me yesterday, she considered him out of danger. Isn't it wonderfully good?"

Of course, the president was far from out of the woods, and the very next day, July 23, Mrs. Blaine reported, "I am just home from the White House…Every one looking very anxious and sober. Mrs. Garfield said the President did not mind much who was in the room with him today." A few days later, on July 29, Garfield met briefly with his Cabinet, the only such meeting held following the shooting.

During his trial, Guiteau would tell the court that "the Deity allowed the Doctors to finish my work gradually," and he was probably correct. Had the doctors left the bullet in place and just kept the wound bandaged and clean, Garfield would almost certainly have survived and had a full recovery. However, in their efforts to locate the bullet, they frequently used dirty fingers or instruments, which introduced infections into Garfield's system that drove his fever up and his appetite down. In the 11 weeks that he lingered following the shooting, the president wasted away before their very eyes, going from 200 to

135 pounds.

As the heat in Washington reached its height, Navy engineers placed fans in the president's room and kept them blowing over large boxes of ice to help keep him cool, and Alexander Graham Bell created a metal detector that would have located the bullet had the president not been lying on a metal bed frame when it was used. However, nothing could stop the infections, which spread and brought on blood poisoning that caused the stricken president to hallucinate and suffer from infected abscesses that broke out all over his body. On August 23, Mrs. Blaine wrote, "I was at the White House last night. Miss Edson abandoned hope. Why, indeed, should that angel tarry longer by that bed when the poor sufferer has lost his own identity, praying to have that other man taken from him away, and to be relieved from that other man's face which cleaves to and drags upon his? About ten, or perhaps later, we came home, when your father penned his bulletin to Lowell." Two days later, she added, "I suppose you can see as well as another that hope is over. Every night I try to brace for that telephone which I am sure before morning will send its shrill summons. The morning is a little reassuring, for light of itself gives courage. Your father I follow upstairs and down like a dog."

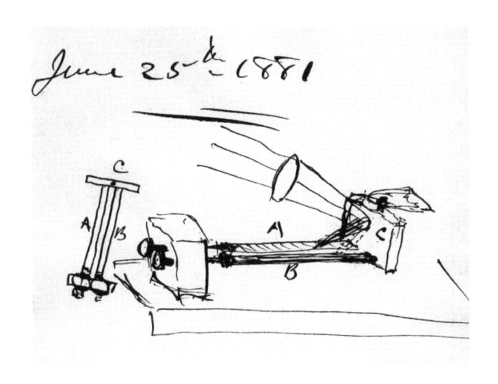

A sketch of Bell's metal detector.

By this time, many began wondering if there was anything that could be done to save the nation's leader. William Chandler, who subsequently became Secretary of the Navy, wrote on August 29, "I have no patience with the fault-finders, and I think Dr. … ought to be suppressed; but I wish the doctors had found out before six weeks had passed where the ball went, and had kept opium out of him, which, combined with the extreme heat of Washington, is likely to prevent his recovery just as it seems evident that he might recover from the direct influence of the ball…. I do not feel as if I ever wanted to set foot in its streets again. I expect to see its effect in the changed looks and gray hairs of my friends who have been there during these anxious weeks."

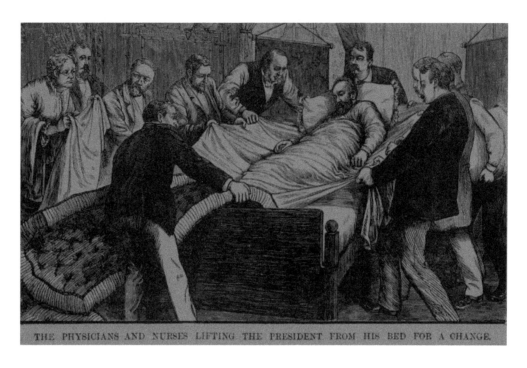

THE PHYSICIANS AND NURSES LIFTING THE PRESIDENT FROM HIS BED FOR A CHANGE.

An illustration depicting Garfield being cared for by nurses and doctors

Finally, on September 6, the doctors decided to allow Garfield to travel with his family to the Jersey Shore, hoping that the cool sea air might help turn the tide in his recovery. Blaine noted, "President left this morning at 6 o'clock. We follow in an hour. I tremble for the experiment and its success, but it was fatal to stay here…" Later, he added, "The President holds his own. I wish I could say a great deal more, but I cannot, and I am overcome with dread of the final result. He is so greatly reduced; still, he has lived out seventy-one days, and that is a great thing. Was there ever a life so desired and so prayed for! May God look down in mercy!"

Sadly, Blaine's prayers, and those of the nation, would

not be answered, at least not in the way they intended. While Garfield rested and enjoyed the cool days at the shore, the infection continued to spread, leading ultimately to blood poisoning, pneumonia and, finally, a burst aneurism that ended his life on September 19, 1881, 80 days after he was shot.

An autopsy was performed the following day, and the report read in part, "It was found that the ball, after fracturing the right eleventh rib, had passed through the spinal column in front of the spinal cord, fracturing the body of the first lumbar vertebra, driving a number of small fragments of bone into the adjacent soft parts, and lodging below the pancreas, about two inches and a half to the left of the spine, and behind the peritoneum, where it had become completely encysted. The immediate cause of death was secondary hemorrhage from one of the mesenteric arteries adjoining the track of the ball, the blood rupturing the peritoneum, and nearly a pint escaping into the abdominal cavity. This hemorrhage is believed to have been the cause of the severe pain in the lower part of the chest complained of just before death. An abscess-cavity, six inches by four in dimensions, was found in the vicinity of the gall-bladder, between the liver and the transverse colon, which were strongly adherent. It did not involve the substance of the liver, and no communication was found between it and the wound. A long, suppurating channel extended from the external wound, between the loin muscles and the right kidney almost to the right groin. This channel, now known to be due to the burrowing of pus from the wound, was supposed, during life, to have been the track of the ball."

In the end, the wound itself was not the ultimate cause of death. The autopsy report explained, "On an examination of the organs of the chest evidences of severe bronchitis were found on both sides, with broncho-pneumonia of the lower portions of the right lung, and, though to a much less extent, of the left. … In reviewing the history of the case in connection with the autopsy, it is quite evident that the different suppurating surfaces, and especially the fractured spongy tissue of the vertebrae, furnish a sufficient explanation of the septic condition which existed."

A picture of Garfield's casket lying in the Capitol
rotunda

THE REMAINS OF PRESIDENT GARFIELD LYING IN STATE IN THE ROTUNDA OF THE CAPITOL AT WASHINGTON

An illustration depicting mourners viewing the body

INTERIOR OF THE GARFIELD RECEIVING VAULT, IN LAKEVIEW CEMETERY, CLEVELAND.

An illustration depicting Garfield's funeral back in Ohio

A contemporary mourning ribbon

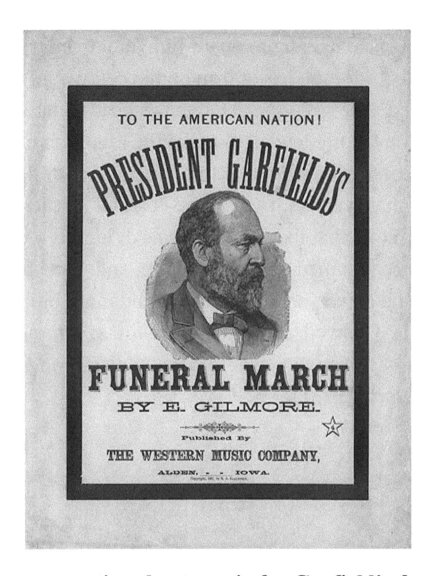

Commemorative sheet music for Garfield's funeral

Chapter 5: Boasting of His Crime

"Meanwhile, the assassin, almost boasting of his crime and waiting for the death, eagerly inquired every day for the news. He declared that it was for the good of the nation that he committed the deed, and pretended to pray for the people. His prison was guarded by police and soldiers to protect him from the mob, for the people regarded him and his act in almost a frenzy of rage. Even one of the sentinels set to guard him attempted to shoot him, and but for the bar of iron on his cell would have succeeded. The ball grazed Guiteau's head. That unlawful attempt on his life tended to make the murderer change his demeanor, and from that time on the fear of death was so great that every footstep in the corridor startled him, and when told that the President was dying his seared conscience assumed again its sceptre, and made him crouch and cower, and call on God and man for mercy." – Russell H. Conwell, *The Life, Speeches, and Public Services of James A. Garfield, Twentieth President of the United States* (1881)

An illustration depicting Guiteau's arraignment in *A Complete History of the Trial of Charles Guiteau*

In the aftermath of the shooting, the police had taken

Guiteau into custody and began trying to make some sense of what he had done, but understandably, this proved to be challenging because Guiteau was unlike anyone else they had ever dealt with. Lieutenant' Eckloff of the Metropolitan Police Headquarters recalled, "When he was brought in we searched him, but he took from his pocket unassisted the pistol that he had used. It was too large for the hip pocket, and he had considerable difficulty in getting it out. He said to us that we need not be excited at all, that if we wanted to know why he did the act we would find it in his papers in the breast pocket of his coat. We took the pistol out of his hand and found it to be a five-shooter, with two barrels empty. It was what is termed an ' English bull-dog,' and carries a ball as large as a navy revolver does."

Detective McElfresh interviewed the suspect on their way to the jail and relayed that their exchange was something along these lines;

McElfresh: "Where are you from ?"

Guiteau: "I am a native-born American; born in Chicago."

McElfresh: "Why did you do this ?"

Guiteau: "I did it to save the Republican party."

McElfresh: "What is your politics?"

Guiteau: "I am a stalwart among the stalwarts. With Garfield out of the way we can carry all the Northern States, and with him in the way we can't carry a single one. Who are you?"

McElfresh: "A detective officer of this department."

Guiteau: "You stick to me and have me put in the third story front at the jail. General Sherman is coming down to take charge. Arthur and all these men are my friends, and I'll have you made Chief of Police. When you get back to the police you will find that I left two bundles of papers at the news stand, which will explain all."

McElfresh: "Is there anybody else with you in this matter?"

Guiteau: "Not a living soul; I contemplated this thing for the last few weeks."

When the men finally arrived at the jail, Guiteau admitted he had been there before: "I was down here last Saturday morning and wanted them to let me look through, and they told me that I could not, but to come on Monday. I wanted, to see what kind of quarters I would have to occupy."

SERGEANT MASON AND THE JAIL WHERE GUITEAU IS CONFINED.—From a Photograph by John Golden and a Sketch by Charles Graham.

A contemporary depiction of the jail where Guiteau was kept

A modern picture of the jail

When the police searched Guiteau, they discovered the letter he had been carrying in his pocket, and it read in part, "July 2, 1881. To the White House: The President's tragic death was a sad necessity, but it will unite the Republican Party and save the Republic. Life is a flimsy dream, and it matters little when one goes; a human life is of small value. During the war thousands of brave boys went down without a tear. I presume the President was a Christian, and that he will be happier in Paradise than here. It will be no worse for Mrs. Garfield, dear soul, to part with her husband this way than by natural death. He is liable to go at any time, anyway. I had no ill-will towards the President. His death was a political necessity. I am a lawyer, a theologian, and a politician…I have some papers for the press, which I shall leave with Byron Andrews and his company, journalists, at No. 1420 New York Avenue, where all the reporters can see them. I am going to the jail. CHARLES GUITEAU."

Like most disturbed people, Guiteau thrived on the attention he was receiving for his deed, and he penned a letter to what he termed "the Chicago Press" announcing that he was writing and would soon publish his autobiography, which would be called *The Life and Theology of Charles Guiteau*. He planned to use the money he made from this book to make bail, after which he could then go on a speaking tour similar to the ones he had done in the past. He assumed that his popularity would now be such that he would make enough money from these tours to hire the best lawyers to defend him and thus be acquitted of the charges brought against him.

Unfortunately for Guiteau, his jailers soon learned of his joy in seeing his name in print and stopped allowing him access to newspapers. This caused the prisoner to become increasingly agitated as the summer wore on. His guards, hardly faring any better in the summer heat, also became more and more irritable, and one of them, William Mason, finally had enough. In a fit of rage, Mason pulled out his side arm and fired at Guiteau, but the bullet hit one of the prison bars instead of the assassin. When the public heard what he had done, the jail was deluged with donations for Mason and his family, but he was still court-martialed for his deed and sentenced to eight years in prison.

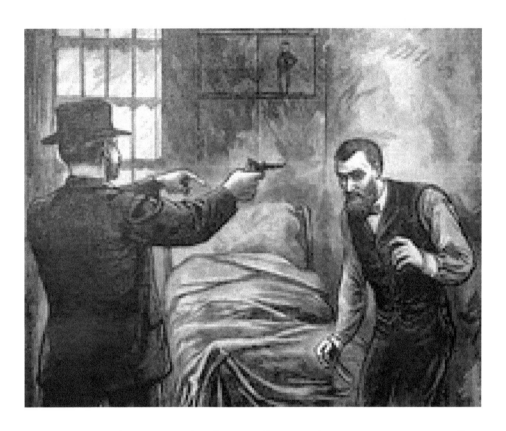

An illustration depicting Mason's attempt to shoot Guiteau

When he learned in September that Garfield had died, Guiteau collapsed and fell to his knees at the magnitude of the event, but he seemed to be back to normal (at least for him) by the following day. He even wrote to the new president, Chester Arthur, that Garfield's death "is a [godsend] to you & I presume you appreciate it. It raises you from $8,000 to $50,000 a year. It raises you from a political cypher to President of the United States with all its powers and honors...." After making some recommendations about cabinet positions, he concluded, "Let all honor be paid to Gen. Garfield's remains. He was a good man but a weak politician."

In October, Guiteau's autobiography, which he dictated from jail, was completed and published in the *New York Herald*, but perhaps not surprisingly, it did not bring him the sort of adulation he had expected as he continued to sit in jail. Meanwhile, George Corkhill, the district attorney who had been tasked with bringing him to justice, was busy preparing to prosecute the assassin. He knew Guiteau's defense attorney was likely to go with an insanity defense, and he would be ready for it.

On October 8, the prosecutor filed an indictment against Guiteau for Garfield's murder, and when Guiteau was arraigned six days later, George Scoville, Guiteau's brother-in-law, appeared on his behalf and was granted a continuance so that he could gather more evidence with which to make his case. Scoville hoped that the time he bought would allow him the ability to bolster the case that Guiteau was insane and that Garfield died as a result of poor medical care. In granting the continuance, Judge Walter Cox set the trial to begin the following month.

Judge Cox

Chapter 6: Grave Responsibility

"The Constitution of the United States provides that 'In all criminal prosecutions the accused shall enjoy the right to a speedy and public trial, by an impartial jury of the state and district wherein the crime shall have been committed; to be informed of the nature and cause of the accusation; to be confronted with the witnesses against him; to have compulsory process for obtaining witnesses in his favor; and to have the assistance of counsel for his defense.' These provisions are deemed the indispensable safeguards of life and liberty. They are intended for the protection of the innocent from injustice and oppression. It is only by their faithful observance that guilt or innocence can be fairly ascertained. Every accused person is presumed innocent until the accusation be proved, and until such proof no court dare to prejudge his cause or withhold from him the protection of this fundamental law. … If he be guilty, no man deserves their protection less than he does. If he be innocent, no man needs their protection more, and no man's case more clearly proves their beneficence and justice. … No one can feel more keenly than I do the grave responsibility of my duty; and I feel that I can only discharge it by a close adherence to the law as it has been laid down by its highest authorized expounders." - Judge Cox's charge to the jury at the end of the trial

St. Elizabeth's Hospital, where Guiteau was housed during his trial

By the time his trial began on November 14, 1881, Guiteau was in high spirits, anxious to be the center of the attention he so craved. He arrived a court dressed conservatively, in a black suit with a white shirt. When given the chance to speak, he asked only that nothing be done to offend "the Deity whose servant I was when I sought to remove the late President." Because of the notoriety of the case, the court found it difficult to find impartial jurors, and the final jury of 12 men included one African-American, a fact that Guiteau object to most strenuously.

From the very beginning, it was clear that Guiteau would not brook any attention falling on anyone other than himself. He began by insisting that he would not accept the representation of any "blunderbuss lawyers" and would instead make his own case, telling the court, "I came in here in the capacity as an agent of the Deity in this matter, and I am going to assert my right in this case."

For his part, Corkhill focused his attention on proving that Guiteau had indeed shot Garfield, and that the bullet had indeed ended the president's life. Dr. D. W. Bliss, who had performed the autopsy, made a most effective witness, using pieces of Garfield's actual vertebrae to demonstrate that the bullet Guiteau fired made the president's death inevitable, no matter how long it might have taken to happen. That afternoon, as Guiteau was being driven away from the courthouse, a drunken farmer named Bill Jones shot at him through the van bars but succeeded only in putting a hole in his coat.

When it came Scoville's turn, he tried to demonstrate to the jurors that his client was insane and should therefore receive treatment rather than punishment, telling them that such a move "is a change all the while progressing to a better state of things, to higher intelligence, to better judgment." However, while he was trying to make his case to the jury, Guiteau continued to interrupt him, repeatedly defending himself against Scoville's descriptions of his past behavior. Guiteau was willing to admit to being insane at the time of the shooting, but only because he believed that God had momentarily removed his free will and made him shoot Garfield, an interesting twist on the more traditional defense that the devil made him do it. Guiteau also believed that the doctors' negligence was primarily responsible for Garfield's death and questioned whether a court in Washington could try him given that the president died in New Jersey.

Scoville was almost certainly correct in determining that his best plan was to focus on the insanity angle, but Dr. John Gray, the superintendent of New York's Utica Asylum and the state's best witness, questioned Guiteau extensively before concluding that he had killed Garfield because of a sense of "wounded vanity and disappointment," not insanity. Then there was the matter of the M'Naghten rule, which required that in order to be found insane, the accused had to be unable to understand that what he did was against the law, and to know the possible consequences of his act. It was clear that Guiteau understood both that shooting Garfield was illegal and that the president might well die from his wounds. Indeed, he frequently testified that Garfield's death was his goal, and Guiteau also made it clear, in writing and on the stand, that he had carefully planned the shooting, so it was clearly not a crime of passion.

Still, Scoville was able to call a number of witnesses to testify of Guiteau's irrational behavior in the days before and after the shooting, and of course, no witness was as much anticipated as the accused himself, who took the stand on November 28, 1881. In the days that followed, first Scoville and then John Porter, a member of the prosecution, questioned him. In making his point that Guiteau did indeed know what he was doing, the latter led him through the plans he made in the days leading up to the shooting, leading Guiteau to testify, "I want it distinctly understood that I did not do that act in my own personality. I unite myself with the Deity, and I want you gentlemen to so understand it. I never should have shot the President on my own personal account. I want that distinctly understood. … The Deity furnished the money by which I bought [the pistol]. I was the agent of the Deity. … I have no objection to stating decidedly that I got $15 of Mr. Maynard's and used $10 of it to buy the pistol with. … It was of no consequence whether I got it from him or somebody else. Mr. Maynard did not know what I wanted the money for. I simply went to him and said, "I owe you $10 and I want to get $15 more, and I will give you a due-bill for the whole." He said to come in, in about fifteen minutes. It was then a quarter to 10 or such a matter, and I came in again and he gave me the money. That is all there is to it. It is of no consequence where I got the money or what I did with it. I do not claim that I was [inspired] to do the specific act; but I claim that the Deity inspired me to remove the President, and I had to use my ordinary judgment as to ways and means to accomplish the Deity's will. The inspiration consisted in trying to remove the President for the good of the American people, and all these details are nothing."

When asked about the ultimate outcome of his actions, Guiteau said, "The whole matter was in the hands of the Deity…. Of course, I appreciate the mere outward fact of the President's disability in his long sickness as much as any person in the world. That is a very narrow view to take of this matter--just the mere outward fact of the President's disability and sickness. I believed that it was the will of God that he should be removed, and that I was the appointed agent to do it."

Then there was the matter of whether or not he should be punished for his actions. On this point, Guiteau asserted, "If I had shot the President of the United States on my own personal account, no punishment would be too severe or too quick for me; but acting as the agent of the Deity puts an entirely different construction upon the act, and that is the thing that I want to put into this court and jury and the opposing counsel. I say this was an absolute necessity, in view of the political situation, for the good of the American people, and to save the nation from another war. That is the view I want you to entertain, and not settle down on a cold-blooded idea of murder. I never had the first conception of his removal as murder. I think the American people may sometime consider themselves under great obligations to me, sir."

At the same time, he maintained that he should not be punished for something over which he had no control: "After I got the conception, my mind was gradually being transformed and fixed as to the necessity of the act. My mind was not fully made up until about two weeks after-- the two weeks I was resisting. I was finding out whether it was the Lord's will or not. Do you understand that? I was finding out whether it was God's will, and at the end I made up my mind that it was His will. That is the way I test the Lord. … I say that the Deity has confirmed the inspiration, thus far, and that He will take care of me. … Anything the Deity does is always right. He directed me to remove the President for the good of the American people. That is the way it always came to my mind. I never had any conception of it being a murder in the ordinary sense. I say the Deity killed the President, and not me. … I do not entertain the idea, sir, that there was any murder in this matter. There is no more murder in this matter than there would be to kill a man during the war. There was a homicide but no murder in it. I do not wish to discuss this matter with you any further, Judge Porter. It is altogether too sacred a matter for you to make light of, and I won't have it. You know my position on that point just as well as if you talked about it six weeks. It is too sacred to be discussed in this foolish, sickening kind of a way."

In spite of his rambling and often strange comments, the prosecution was able to get him to admit that there was much about his preparations for his deed that were obviously rational, including purchasing the pistol. Guiteau admitted, "I saw the pistol, and I noticed it the first time in a show-case. I saw a lot of pistols exposed for sale, and I saw this particular one, and I looked at it. … I am no expert on fire-arms at all, and never had a pistol before in my life, and knew nothing about using it. The man loaded it for me and I put it in my pocket. … I went out in the street. I do not know where I went with it." When he was questioned about why he knew to practice with the firearm before using it, Guiteau insisted, "I wanted to fire it off two or three times, as I knew nothing about a weapon, and I expected to be obliged to use it, and I wanted to familiarize myself with the outward uses of the weapon. I knew nothing about it, no more than a child."

This intrigued Parker and led to the following exchange:

"Q: You did not know how to shoot a pistol?

A: I knew nothing about it at all.

Q: But it was the Deity that was to shoot; didn't He know how?

A: There is no use of your whining in that kind of way; you may as well rest on that. You are making altogether too much talk about the mere outward act. I wish your mind to go back and look at the motive; the motive is what we are looking at.

Q: The motive was to kill, was it not?

A: To remove the President of the United States for the good of the American people, and the mere outward fact of how and when and where are all irrelevant matters. There is no use of your whining on this kind of talk any more."

Then there was the matter of his personal reasons for wanting the President dead, specifically that he had overlooked Guiteau in handing out jobs and that Guiteau hoped to use his new found notoriety to sell more books. The defendant admitted, "I should have removed the President any time from about the middle of June until I actually shot him if I had had an opportunity. …It was perfectly clear from the 1st of June, but I was not actually ready to do the act until about the middle of June. I had a good deal to do in the two weeks after the 1st of June until about the middle of June getting ready. For instance, I went to work and revised my book, The Truth. I knew there would be some demand for that. I also did several other matters, personal to myself, that I had to attend to; so, as a matter of fact, any time from the middle of June until the 2d of July if I had had an opportunity at the President, I should have shot him. I was watching for the opportunity during those two weeks. At any time during those two weeks I should have executed the divine will if I had had an opportunity…. I say that the entire responsibility of that thing is on the Deity; that He has taken care of it thus far, and that He will continue to take care of it. … The Deity uses certain men to serve Him. He is using this honorable court, and this jury, and all these policemen, and these troops to serve Him and to protect me."

Guiteau on the witness stand. *Harper's Weekly*

As far as the Deity's reasons for wanting Garfield dead, Guiteau insisted, "That was the misconduct of the President. He had gone back on Grant and Conkling and Arthur, the very men that carried New York, and without which he could not have been elected, and he then put himself right under the influence of Mr. Blaine."

Throughout his testimony, Guiteau repeatedly claimed that he did not see the dead president as a bad man, and that he in fact believe he was at that time in heaven: "No doubt he is a great deal happier now at this very moment than any man that is on earth. I presume he was a Christian man; I have no doubt of it at all. I think his Christian character had nothing whatever to do with his political record. Please put that down. His political record was, in my opinion, very poor; but his Christian character was good. Garfield was a good man, as far as I know, although they used to tell very hard stories about him on the Credit Mobilier business, and all that I don't know whether it was true or not. In my speech I defended him on that matter. Many papers were denouncing him as a thief and a Credit Mobilier rascal, and all that sort of thing, and we had fought very strongly against the attacks made upon him."

Of course, there was always the question in some people's minds as to whether or not some sort of conspiracy was afoot. While Guiteau denied any sort of understanding with Arthur about what he was going to do, he still wanted to point out his own importance: "I considered General Arthur my friend at that time, and do now. …I was with him every day and night during the canvass in New York. … I mean to say that when I went up to see General Arthur, I went right into his room. …he had his private room, and only those who were supposed to be his personal friends were admitted. He had two or three rooms, and the crowd stayed back." Parker then asked him specifically, "You never had any conversation with him about murder, did you?" Guiteau replied, "No, sir; I did not. Neither he or General Grant knew anything about this inspiration."

Scoville's only hope to undo the damage done by Guiteau's own testimony was to bring in medical experts who could demonstrate that the man could not have known what he was doing when he shot the president. However, this proved to be a challenge. Dr. James Kienarn, a respected neurologist out of Chicago, explained to the jury that a man could indeed be insane without the accompanying delusions that were commonly believed to indicate mental disability. However, his testimony proved less than helpful once the prosecution got him to admit that he believed 20% or more of the population was either insane or one day would be. The defense called seven more doctors, but none of them seemed very effective.

Scoville had one last chance when he called a New York neurologist named Dr. Edward Spitzka to the stand. Spitzka testified extensively to Guiteau's obvious insanity until, under cross-examination, he was forced to admit that he was not actually a neurologist but instead a veterinarian. Almost 20 years later, Spitzka would participate in the autopsy of Leon Czolgosz, the anarchist who assassinated President William McKinley in September 1901.

EDWARD CHARLES SPITZKA, M.D.
PHYSICIAN AND BIOLOGIST
ALIENIST. WRITER ON MENTAL AND SPINAL DISEASES

Spitzka

In response to the defense's now thoroughly trounced witnesses, the prosecution introduced Dr. Fordyce Barker, who told the court "there was no such disease in science as hereditary insanity" and that those who could not control themselves were in the throes of vice, not insanity.

Dr. Noble Young, the prison's own physician, told the jury the Guiteau was not only "perfectly sane" but also "as bright and intelligent a man as you will ever see in a summer's day." Finally, Gray took the stand and made it clear that, following two days of interviewing Guiteau, he was certain that Guiteau, while depraved, was also sane.

Chapter 7: An Excuse for Crime

"But, in order to constitute the crime of murder, the assassin must have a responsibly sane mind. The technical term, 'sound memory and discretion,' in the old common-law definition of murder, means this. An irresponsibly insane man can no more commit murder than a sane man can do so without killing. His condition of mind cannot be separated from the act. If he is laboring under disease of his mental faculties -- if that is a proper expression -- to such an extent that he does not know what he is doing, or does not know that it is wrong, then he is wanting in that sound memory and discretion which make a part of the definition of murder. … In the next place, notwithstanding this presumption of innocence, it is equally true that a defendant is presumed to be sane and have been so at the time when the crime charged against him was committed; that is to say, the government is not bound, as a part of its proofs, to show, affirmatively, that the defendant was sane. As insanity is the exception, and most men are sane, the law presumes the latter condition of everybody until some reason is shown to believe the contrary. The burden is therefore on the defendant, who sets up insanity as an excuse for crime, to bring forward his proofs, in the first instance, to show that that presumption is a mistake as far as it relates to him." - Judge Cox

Finally, on January 15, 1882, Guiteau got his long awaited chance to speak directly to the jury. He began, "I am going to sit down, because I can talk. I am not afraid of anyone shooting me. This shooting business is declining. I am not here as a wicked man, or as a lunatic, I am here as a patriot and my speech is as follows. I read from the New York Herald, gentlemen. It was sent by telegraph Sunday, and published in all the leading papers in America Monday. If the court please, gentlemen of the jury: I am a patriot. Today I suffer in bonds as a patriot. Washington was a patriot. Grant was a patriot. Washington led the armies of the Revolution through eight years of bloody war to victory and glory. Grant led the armies of the Union to victory and glory, and today the nation is prosperous and happy. They raised the old way-cry, 'Rally round the flag, boys,' and thousands of the choicest sons of the Republic went forth to battle, to victory or death. Washington and Grant, by their valor and success in war, won the admiration of mankind. Today I suffer in bonds as a patriot, because I had the inspiration and nerve to unite a great political party, to the end that the nation might be saved another desolating war. In the grief and mourning that followed President Garfield's death, all contention ceased..."

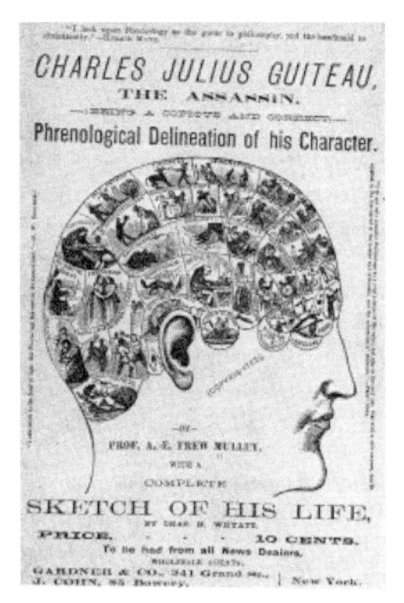

A brochure published about Guiteau during his trial

He then reviewed his earlier statements while he had testified, namely that he did nothing to Garfield out of anger or malice, and that ultimately the president died due to the poor treatment he received from his doctors. While this is now obviously true, no one at that time could have known that with any certainty, and of course, had he not shot Garfield in the first place, the president would not have died.

Guiteau also brought up the issue of political disagreements in the United States, and his belief that with Garfield gone, these would be rectified. He even went so far as to read aloud "fan mail" that had been sent to him thanking him for his deed. He then returned to his topic, saying, "As sure as you are alive, gentlemen, as sure as you are alive, if a hair of my head is harmed this nation will go down to desolation... all you can do is put my body in the ground, but this nation will pay for it as sure as you are alive. To hang a man in my mental condition on July 2 would be a lasting disgrace to the American people; they did not want the Republican party's savior hung. The mothers and daughters of the republic are praying that your will vindicate my inspiration, and their prayers I expect will prevail. A woman's instinct is keener than man's, and I pray you listen to the prayers of these ladies."

10 days later, when Judge Cox gave his charge to the jury, he made his feelings about Guiteau's ramblings very clear: "Before proceeding, I wish to interject here a

remark upon an episode in the trial pending the last argument. The prisoner has taken repeated occasions to proclaim that public opinion, as evidenced by the press and by his correspondence, is in his favor. As you well know, these declarations could not have been prevented except by resorting to the process of gagging him. Any suggestion that you could be influenced by this lawless babble of the prisoner, would have seemed to me simply absurd, and I should have felt that I had almost insulted your intelligence if I had warned you not to regard it. The counsel for the prosecution have been rebuked for allowing these declarations to go to you without contradiction, and in the course of the final argument they felt it necessary to interpose a contradiction to these declarations of the prisoner, and the latter's counsel excepted to the form in which the contradiction was made. For the sole purpose of purging this record of any apparently objectionable matter, I would simply say, here, that nothing that has been said in reference to public sentiment or newspaper opinion, on either side, is to be regarded by you, although I really feel that such an admonition from me is totally unnecessary."

The judge then talked extensively about the need for proof and other factors they were to consider, finally handing them the case as the sun was setting on January 25, 1882. In just over an hour, the jury was back and the foreman, John P. Hamlin, announced that they had found Guiteau guilty. Upon hearing that, Guiteau cried out, "My blood be on the head of that jury; don't you forget it. That is my answer…God will avenge this outrage." When Cox sentenced him "to be hanged by the neck until you are dead," Guiteau replied, "I had rather stand where I am than where the jury does or where your Honor does."

JURY THAT CONVICTED GUITEAU.

Judge Cox and the jury

By the end of May, Guiteau had exhausted all his appeals, and a month later, on June 22, President Arthur heard his plea for a stay of execution but refused it. Guiteau complained, "Arthur has sealed his own doom and the doom of this nation."

For Guiteau, the day of his execution offered him the chance to give a final performance, and he was determined to make the most of his last moment in the spotlight. Mounting the gallows on June 30, 1882, he danced his way up to the scaffolding and then read 14 Bible verses. After that, he concluded with a poem he had composed for the occasion:

"I am going to the Lordy, I am so glad, I am going to the Lordy, I am so glad,
I am going to the Lordy, Glory hallelujah! Glory hallelujah!
I am going to the Lordy. I love the Lordy with all my soul, Glory hallelujah!
And that is the reason I am going to the Lord, Glory hallelujah! Glory hallelujah!
I am going to the Lord. I saved my party and my land, Glory hallelujah!
But they have murdered me for it, And that is the reason

"I am going to the Lordy, Glory hallelujah! Glory hallelujah!
I am going to the Lordy! I wonder what I will do when I get to the Lordy,
I guess that I will weep no more When I get to the Lordy! Glory hallelujah!
I wonder what I will see when I get to the Lordy, I expect to see most glorious things,
Beyond all earthly conception When I am with the Lordy! Glory hallelujah! Glory hallelujah!
I am with the Lord."

As these last words were spoken, the executioner pulled

the lever and Guiteau fell, putting an end to one of the most tragic episodes in American history.

The McKinley Assassination

Chapter 1: The Scene of the Assassination

"The scene of the assassination was the Temple of Music, at the Exposition grounds. The day previous was Presidents day at the Exposition, and President McKinley had delivered what many believed to be the greatest speech of his life. Praises for his wisdom and statesmanship were ringing around the world. On the fateful day the President attended the Exposition as a visitor, and in the afternoon held a reception in the Temple of Music. The reception to the President was one to which the general public had been invited. President John G. Milburn of the Exposition had introduced the President to the great crowd in. the Temple, and men, women and children came forward for a personal greeting. Among those in line was Leon Czolgosz, whose right hand was wrapped in a handkerchief. Folded in the handkerchief was a 32-caliber self-acting-revolver holding five bullets. A little girl was led up by her father and the President shook hands with her. As she passed along to the right the President looked after her smilingly and waved his hand in a pleasant adieu." – Marshall Everett, *Complete life of William McKinley and story of his assassination. An authentic and official memorial edition, containing every incident in the career of the immortal statesman, soldier, orator and patriot*

Friday, September 6, 1901, dawned bright and clear for William McKinley, both literally and figuratively. Just months after he had been reelected as President of the United States, he was looking forward to the enjoyable duty of once again visiting the Pan American Exposition, a symbol of all he believed the country was and could be.

McKinley

That morning's timetable called for him to visit the Temple of Music. According to one exposition guide, "The Temple of Music is the center for musical interests at the Exposition. Its architecture is a free treatment of the Spanish Renaissance, it being octagonal in form, with pavilions at the corners. The grand entrance is at the corner of the Esplanade and Court of Fountains, the spacious courts upon which most of the principal buildings of the Exposition have their frontage. The cornice and balustrade are of elaborate composition, the latter bearing names familiar to the musical world. The interior of the temple is particularly fine in its sculptural and color decorations. The exterior of the building is ornate in architectural features and groups of sculpture designed to illustrate the purpose and character of the building. The great organ in the Temple of Music was built by Emmons Howard of Westfield, Mass., and cost $15,000. Concerts are held in the Temple every afternoon and evening. They are of a varied nature, but the high standard is maintained throughout. There are three band stands on the Exposition grounds, one in the rear, or north of the Electric Tower, in the center of the Sunken Gardens, and two in the Grand Esplanade, which will hold 250,000 people. Upwards of twenty bands have been employed to furnish music during the Exposition."

A postcard depicting the Temple of Music

A picture of the Temple of Music taken at the expo

McKinley had other reasons to be optimistic about the day, as he was still riding the tidal wave of applause he had received the previous day for what many considered to be his greatest speech. In it, he had praised the exposition and all like it, saying, "The quest for trade is an incentive to men of business to devise, invent, improve and economize in the cost of production. Business life, whether among ourselves or with other people, is ever a sharp struggle for success. It will be none the less so in the future. Without competition we would be clinging to the clumsy and antiquated processes of farming and manufacture and the methods of business of long ago, and the twentieth would be no further advanced than the eighteenth century. But though commercial competitors we are, commercial enemies we must not be. The Pan-American Exposition has done its work thoroughly, presenting in its exhibits evidences of the highest skill and illustrating the progress of the human family in the western hemisphere. This portion of the earth has no cause for humiliation for the part it has performed in the march of civilization. It has not accomplished everything; far from it. It has simply done its best, and without vanity or boastfulness and recognizing the manifold achievements of others, it invites the friendly rivalry of all the powers in the peaceful pursuits of trade and commerce, and will co-operate with all in advancing the highest and best interests of humanity."

A picture of McKinley taken on September 5, 1901

Trade was important to McKinley, who had built his presidency on pulling the United States out of its first major economic depression. The Panic of 1893, occurring just a few years before he came into office, had caused serious problems for the nation, which was still recovering from the depths of the Civil War. Indeed, one of the men in Buffalo that day, anarchist Leon Czolgosz, had lost his job during the Panic of 1893, which drove him towards embracing anarchy in the first place. Thanks in large measure to McKinley's guidance, however, the country was once again on solid economic ground and experiencing the type of boom that typically only comes along once or twice in a generation.

Czolgosz

Presidential security in 1901 was quite lax by modern standards. For instance, while in Buffalo, the president and his wife stayed at the house of John Milburn, the president of the exposition. McKinley enjoyed the informality of someone's home and, always solicitous of his wife, felt that Ida was more comfortable away from prying eyes, but while the Secret Service had no problem securing the home, some felt that having the president walk around the fairgrounds with the rest of the crowds was not a good idea. George Cortelyou, McKinley's personal secretary, was particularly concerned about the President's visit to the Temple of Music and repeatedly tried to have that stop removed from the program altogether, but McKinley insisted on putting it back in. Defeated but not deterred, Cortelyou telegraphed the exposition staff and had them arrange extra security for McKinley's tour of the Temple.

Ida McKinley

Cortelyou

JOHN G. MILBURN
PRESIDENT OF THE PAN-AMERICAN EXPOSITION.

Milburn

The Milburn house

By the time he arrived at the Temple of Music, McKinley and his wife had enjoyed a tour of Niagara Falls and returned by train to Buffalo. Ida was not feeling well and decided not to accompany her husband to the public reception at the Temple, but McKinley arrived there at around 4:00 p.m., basking in the glow of applause as those in line waited to shake his hand.

Randolph Keim was there that day and had a good view of the events that subsequently transpired. The next day, he recorded his observations, beginning with a description of the president's arrival: "Hearing the cheers of the vast throng of people who were awaiting the arrival of the President at the exposition grounds, I sauntered across the esplanade to view the enthusiastic demonstrations which were being made as the procession passed along the western drive of the esplanade in a southerly direction from the railroad gate. The Presidential party arrived at the Music Temple about three minutes past 4 o'clock, entering the northeast doorway. About five minutes later those who had passed before the President began to emerge from the opposite door. I entered the southwest door to witness the form and arrangements for handling such an immense crowd, having been familiar with the long-established custom at the Executive Mansion in Washington. I was in a position to have a full view what was taking place. I was especially attracted by the curved aisle extending diagonally across the floor of the building, the…settees having blue cambric hanging down their backs to make a lane or aisle so that no one could stop. I saw that many of the Park police were stationed along this lane to hasten people out. … Seemingly, thinking a change of form was necessary I was looking directly at the party and noticed Secretary Cortelyou at the rear and back of the receiving party, and who was moving from place to place evidently uneasy."

A picture of McKinley arriving at the Temple of Music

Chapter 2: The Blackest Friday

"On Friday, September 6, 1901, the blackest Friday in American history, the American people were shocked and stunned by the news that their beloved President, William McKinley, had been shot down by a cowardly assassin, while attending the Pan-American Exposition at Buffalo. It was like a flash of lightning from a clear sky. The people were stunned into momentary silence. The sign of grief was on the face of every loyal American, and the hearts of the people beat as one in sympathy for the stricken chief. The horror of the tragic event grew when it was learned that the assassin was an anarchist, and not an insane man as was first supposed. Then came the full realization that the murderous bullet of the assassin was aimed not only at the foremost citizen of the Republic, but that the Red Thing called Anarchy had raised its blood-stained hand against government, against all peaceable authority and law. It was a blow struck at all the institutions of society that men hold dear and sacred. With that wonderful self-control that distinguishes the American people, loyal citizens restrained the rising passion in their breasts, and their suppressed rage was further held in check by the word of hope which followed that the President was yet alive. Alas! it was but a hope, destined to linger but a few days." – Marshall Everett, *Complete life of William McKinley and story of his assassination. An authentic and official memorial edition, containing every incident in the career of the immortal statesman, soldier, orator and patriot*

A picture of McKinley greeting people at the Temple of Music minutes before he was shot

Unfortunately, Cortelyou was right to be worried, because not everyone there that day wished him well. In addition to a handful of people who might have disagreed with his politics or disapproved of him personally, there was one man who truly wished him harm. Leon Czolgosz was an anarchist who had come to believe that the only way to improve America was to get rid of the current president. According to one of the doctors who examined him following the assassination, "Czolgosz may be described as a well-nourished, rather good looking, mild-mannered young man with a pleasant facial expression; features, regular; face, smooth-shaven and symmetrical; mouth and ears well-formed and symmetrical; teeth, none missing, but in poor condition from neglect; …hair, light brown and slightly curly; stature, medium — five feet seven and a half inches — and weight — estimated — about 140 pounds. The extremities were in all respects normal. … There were no signs of specific nodes or periosteal tenderness over the usual sites of these lesions, nor was there any evidence upon the head or body of traumatism, excepting a slight deviation of the nose due to a blow which he received at the time of the assassination, and a superficial, perpendicular cicatrix on the left face which he said was the result of a slight injury he received when working in a barbed wire factory. There were no tremors or twitchings of the facial muscles, tongue or hands."

While there was nothing wrong with him physically, Czolgosz's mental state was quite agitated that afternoon. He had decided a few days earlier that he would come to the exposition to kill the president.

As Czolgosz approached McKinley, some nearest him may have noticed that his right hand was wrapped in a handkerchief. This was not unusual at the time since most men carried handkerchiefs, and anyone who saw him may very well have thought he might have cut his hand on something while touring the exposition.

What no one could see was that the handkerchief concealed not a wound but a .32-caliber revolver leaded with five bullets. According to one report published shortly after the shooting, "The man with the bandaged hand and innocent face received no attention from the detectives beyond the mental observation that his right hand was apparently injured, and that he would present his left hand to the President. The President smiled and presented his right hand in a position to meet the left of the approaching man. Hardly a foot of space intervened between the bodies of the two men. Before their hands met two pistol shots rang out, and the President turned slightly to the left and reeled. The bandage on the hand of the tall, innocent looking young man had concealed a revolver. He had fired through the bandage without removing any portion of the handkerchief. … The first bullet entered too high for the purpose of the assassin, who had fired again as soon as his finger could move the trigger. On receiving the first shot President McKinley lifted himself on his toes with something of a gasp. His movement caused the second shot to enter just below the navel. With the second shot the President doubled slightly forward and then sank back. Secret Service Detective Geary caught the President in his arms and President

Milburn helped to support him. When the President fell into the arms of Detective Geary he coolly asked: 'Am I shot?' Geary unbuttoned the President's vest, and, seeing blood, replied: 'I fear you are, Mr. President.'"

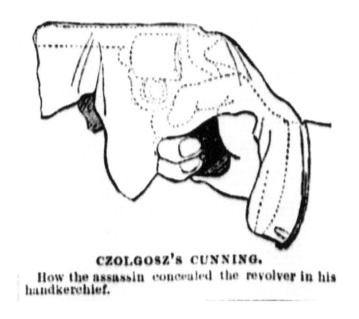

CZOLGOSZ's CUNNING.

How the assassin concealed the revolver in his handkerchief.

A contemporary illustration of the way Czolgosz concealed the gun

A picture of the spot where McKinley was shot (marked with an X)

Keim was nearby, tragically close to all that happened, and he was also very observant. Accustomed to the political environment, he was unhindered by any sense of awe in his surroundings, and from his vantage point, he observed, "Suddenly hearing two quick, sharp reports, and seeing smoke, I feared that something serious had happened. I saw the President fall back (not fall over) and apparently caught by two persons one on each side. I think Mr. Cortelyou was one. I am not sure about the second one. On the impulse of the moment I rushed forward. In an instant the park guard, stationed along the passageway, seemingly about twenty five feet apart, shouted: 'The President is shot! Put everybody out!' Close the doors!

Realizing what had happened, and, observing Secretary Cortelyou and Mr. Millburn and George Foster, of the Secret Service, in attendance, with others, assisting the President, I broke through the improvised aisle…hastily turned around and arranged a settee for the President to rest upon. The President was led forward, along the aisle toward the center of the building walking with great composure, supported by Secretary Cortelyou and Mr. Foster. As he approached the settee, I assisted in placing him upon it. The President sat down with entire self-possession. I began fanning him with my straw hat. Others then began to gather and also fanned him. The President was but slightly pale, and showed little if any signs of nervousness. At this moment the Coast guards and Secret Service men rushed by, carrying the would-be assassin hanging limp in their grasp to the outer entrance to await the patrol wagon. I have since learnt that they took him to a room adjoining the stage."

At first, it was unclear how badly wounded McKinley was. Some hoped that he might have only been grazed, while others feared that his death was imminent. What was clear was that he needed immediate medical care, and an ambulance was sent for at once.

In the meantime, the President was placed in a chair, and according to one report, "His eyes were open and he was clearly conscious of all that had transpired. He looked up into President Milburn s face and gasped: 'Cortelyou,' the name of his private secretary. The President's secretary bent over him. 'Cortelyou,' said the President, 'my wife, be careful about her; don t let her know.' Moved by a paroxysm he writhed to the left and then his eyes fell on the prostrate form of the assassin, Czolgosz, lying on the floor bloody and help less beneath the blows of the guard. The President raised his right hand, red with his own blood, and placed it on the shoulder of his secretary. 'Let no one hurt him,' he gasped, and sank back in the chair, while the guards carried Czolgosz out of his sight."

Keim continued to linger nearby, and though he must have felt some of the same shock that those around him were experiencing, he remembered vivid details of the scene: "The white vest which the President wore had been unbuttoned as well as his shirt front evidently by someone before he was led from the receiving party and showed plainly the powder marks and bullet hole. A little blood had accumulated which attracted the President's eye. It seemed to worry him, somewhat. Secretary Cortelyou, who had now left for a moment to make arrangements for the President's removal, returned. He asked the President: 'Have you much pain?' The President replied, 'No,' turning his head toward the place he had just left and where he had been receiving. Secretary Cortelyou then departed for a second time, and upon returning the

President remarked: 'Let no exaggerated reports reach Mrs. McKinley.' (This is exactly as given, all other reports are incorrect.) This he repeated, while Secretary Cortelyou assured him that his wishes would be carried out. In the meantime, occupying a seat on the settee near the President, I kept fanning him so that he might have plenty of fresh air, as did others some five or six in number who had gathered."

Fortunately, the exposition had a field hospital on its grounds, and even an electrically powered ambulance. Though both these items were designed primarily for show, they were fully operational and soon called into use. Keim continued, "Secretary Cortelyou again departed but reappeared when the stretcher arrived with the hospital aids. This was not more than eight minutes after the atrocious deed had been committed and seemed a remarkably quick response to the call, as not more than five minutes has elapsed. Secretary Cortelyou, and I think George Foster, and myself, with the aid of others, assisted the President, who showed the same self-control as all through the terrible ordeal, to the stre[t]cher. He was covered with a blanket by the hospital attendants and willing hands bore him along the aisle to the ambulance, which was waiting at the outer or southwest door. I carried the upper left hand corner, and, having picked up the President's hat from the settee, where he had placed it, and would evidently have been left, I shielded his face from public gaze as we emerged into the light. As we reached the exterior of the building moans and sobs were distinctly heard from the crowd which had gathered and were held back by the police."

A picture of the ambulance

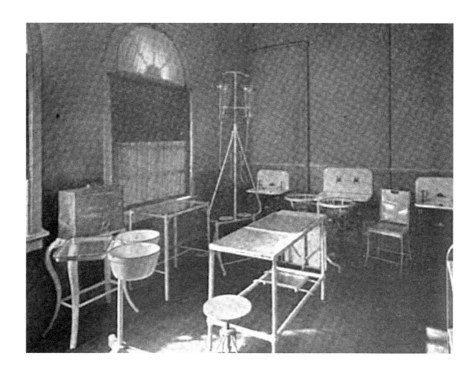

A picture of the operating room in the expo's hospital

As is so often the case when someone famous is injured, there was a great deal of jockeying for position among those who were in charge of caring for him. This was not, to be charitable, primarily a matter of pride but more a matter of each man believing that his leader needed him to be near, and perhaps no man that day felt as responsible for McKinley as Cortelyou. According to Keim, "After the President had been comfortably adjusted in the electric ambulance Secretary Cortelyou desired to ride on the front seat with the driver, but the later objected, not knowing who Mr. Cortelyou was and pushed Mr. Cortelyou off. I said to him (the driver): 'This is the President's secretary and must go!' where upon I pushed Mr. Cortelyou on just as the taller of the attending doctors got up to his seat on the other side evidently because he had not left his seat. This I think now, is the chief service I rendered, for if the ambulance had hurried off Mr. Cortelyou might not have reached the hospital as soon as he did and taken such control of the situation. As the ambulance started, finding no guard on the rear step, I jumped on myself to prevent the door from flying open. There were two hospital attendants on the box with Mr. Cortelyou, and the other riding inside with George Foster. The only government officials accompanying the ambulance were Secretary Cortelyou and myself unless Mr. Foster could be called one. The mounted police, numbering about fifteen, instantly closed in on the rear, and a rapid space was made through the esplanade to the exposition hospital, going north along the west side of the Court of Honor, upon the concrete, and then turned west near the main or west Amherst gate entrance. The smooth concrete payvments [pavement] and the rubber tires ground vibration to a minimum. Many people whom we passed had evidently, as yet, no knowledge of what had transpired within the building."

Chapter 3: Doctors Were at the President's Side

"Six doctors were at the President's side within thirty seconds after his arrival at the hospital, among them the President's family physician, Dr. P. M. Rixey. Dr. Roswell Park, a surgeon of national reputation, was summoned from Niagara Falls, where he was performing an operation, and Dr. Herman Mynter arrived soon after. The surgeons consulted and hesitated about performing an operation. The President reassured them by expressing his confidence, but no decision was reached when Dr. Mann of the exposition hospital staff arrived. After another consultation Dr. Mann informed the President that an operation was necessary. 'All right,' replied the President. 'Go ahead. Do whatever is proper.' The anesthetic administered was ether, and for two and a half hours the President was under the influence of this. The wound in the breast proved to be only a flesh wound. The bullet struck a button and was somewhat deflected. It entered the middle of the breast above the breast bone, but did not penetrate far. When the President was undressed for the operation the bullet fell from his clothing upon the table. The second and serious wound was a bullet hole in the abdomen, about five inches below the left nipple and an inch and a half to the left of the median line. The bullet which caused that wound penetrated both the interior and posterior walls of the stomach, going completely through that organ." – Marshall Everett, *Complete life of William McKinley and story of his assassination. An authentic and official memorial edition, containing every incident in the career of the immortal statesman, soldier, orator and patriot*

Dr. Rixey

Once the party arrived at the hospital, Cortelyou again took the lead. Keim recalled, "Upon halting at the hospital entrance, Secretary Cortelyou was, I think, the first to alight. In the meantime I opened the rear doors, assisted by the young doctor from within the ambulance and

George Foster, having been joined by others, the President was borne into the room on the right of the hall, with ample sunlight, and equipped with the most modern surgical appliances. Shortly several surgeons and physicians arrived. Many others on the outside, in vain sought admittance. I think the accompanying doctors told Mr. Cortelyou who was in charge of the Hospital and which city surgeons were of pronounced ability. One or two others came in and I think Dr. Mynter were accepted."

McKinley was taken to the onsite hospital, where he was immediately surrounded by doctors called in following the shooting. Surgery was still in its early stages, but these men were well-trained, particularly in the treatment of bullet wounds. After a brief but intense conversation, they agreed that surgery was called for, and soon, primarily so they could ascertain the extent of the injuries and whether or not the stomach's contents had entered and thus contaminated the abdominal cavity. Keim explained, "In about fifteen minutes, the time being about 4:45 p.m., Dr. Mann arrived. A hurried examination of the President's wound was made, followed by a consultation in the hall, at which an immediate operation was determined upon. Dr. Mann, who came out into the hall told Mr. Cortelyou (in my hearing),'I think we better operate at once' (these are the very words used), to which Secretary Cortelyou assented. Dr. Park came when the operation had progressed about 20 minutes and Dr. Mann explained what he had determined upon and done thus far. While the doctors were washing up preparatory to the trying operation several telegrams were handed in the side or rear windows and I saw the maid take them asking for Mr. Cortelyou, 'who is Mr. Cortelyou?' &c. I seized them and hurriedly went to Mr. Cortelyou, who, after reading them said to me 'I'll not answer any of them now.' In the meantime, at Secretary Cortelyou's request, I stationed myself at one of the doors of the operating room, with George Foster at the other, with instructions not to permit any undesirable persons to pass. Shortly Mr. Foster retired leaving me the only doorkeeper. In the meantime, by the rear entrance to the hospital, several physicians had entered and were pressing their claims. This entrance was quickly barred and several policemen were stationed there with instructions which I gave. During these moments of waiting, the President, while resting on the operating table was heard to say: 'Thy will be done; thy kingdom come', evidently a sentence from the Lord's prayer, and was, I thought, his prayer at the moment. Other broken words followed. I believe he also said: 'God forgive him - he little knew what he was doing.'"

Keim knew little of the details of the surgery, but he was very familiar with the surgical center: "The operating room was most wonderfully provided with modern appliances, and very timely there was scarcely anything lacking: the glass water jars [interpolation illegible], the glass side boards, the excellent planned two west windows letting in the warm setting sun, light and ventilation, the glass trays with instruments lying in solution of antiseptics, the many kinds of antiseptic bandages, the nurses constantly flying in and out bringing what was required without noise and seemingly without instructions all went to show the thoroughness with which this hospital was fitted."

Later, more details of the surgery itself would come out. According to a contemporary report, "The operation lasted almost an hour. A cut about five inches long was made. It was found necessary to turn up the stomach of the President in order to trace the course of the bullet. The bullet s opening in the front wall of the stomach was small and it was carefully closed with sutures, after which a search was made for the hole in the back wall of the stomach. This hole, where the bullet went out of the stomach, was larger than the hole in the front wall of the stomach; in fact, it was a wound over an inch in diameter, jagged and ragged. It was sewed up in three layers. This wound was larger than the wound where the bullet entered the stomach, because the bullet, in its course, forced tissues through ahead of it. In turning up the stomach, an act that was absolutely necessary, and was performed by Dr. Mann with rare skill, the danger was that some of the contents of the stomach might go into the abdominal cavity, and as a result cause peritonitis. It so happened that there was little in the Presidents' stomach at the time of the operation. Moreover, subsequent developments tended to show that this feature of the operation was successful and that none of the contents of the stomach entered the abdominal cavity. If any of the contents had entered the cavity the probability is that peritonitis would have set in."

While the doctors were operating, the men outside the surgical room were busy organizing the affairs of the nation. Congress was informed of what had happened, and word of the shooting spread like wildfire through Buffalo, but it was still considered imperative that Ida McKinley be kept in the dark until there was some real news to report, so someone was dispatched to the Milburn home to make sure no one brought her news until after the surgery was over. Keim wrote, "During the operation Secretary Cortelyou was in and out of the room observing the progress of the operation receiving numerous telegrams from all parts of the world and answering urgent calls at the main entrance. Throughout he was as cool and collected as if in the ordinary transaction of business in his office at Washington. His coolness under the terrible strain of the situation was the admiration of all. It allayed undue haste or excitement, and at the same time no moments were lost in indecision. It was undoubtedly due to his extraordinary presence of mind that the President's sufferings were reduced to a minimum. … Before the operation George Foster showed the first or stray bullet, and I wondered as I examined it, how so little a missal [missile] could do so much harm as it seemed to have done. It was an ordinary 32 calibre lead bullet uninjured. As darkness drew on the doctors called for more light. So the overhead electric cluster was turned on, later they asked for a movable light. One was produced and I handed it to Dr. Rixey who held it in as required by the surgeons. As the President's clothes were removed before the operation by the regular attendants, Mr. Foster took charge of them and carried them to the front office, where they were locked up. In the meantime, I had charge of the President's hat, but soon afterwords [sic] placed it with the other articles under Mr. Foster's care. At the close of the operation Dr. Parker said 'Gentlemen before we depart I want to say one thing – let nothing that has been seen or heard in this room be repeated.'"

Chapter 4: Improvement in His Condition

"Before the doctors appeared, Secretaries Smith, Wilson, and Hitchcock came out of the house, followed by Secretaries Hay and Root. They said the doctors were still engaged in their consultation, and had not come down stairs. They had been informed, though, they said, that the satisfactory conditions still continued. Very soon after the doctors had left the morning visitors began coming. … They all expressed themselves as confident of the outcome. The bulletin of the physicians was not taken to indicate anything serious, and the visitors confirmed the hopefulness of the situation. The President showed so much improvement in his condition the people began to send flowers to him. Shortly before noon Tuesday a wagon load of flowers arrived at the Milburn house, the gift of Governor Gregory of Rhode Island to the President. They were accompanied by a message of the tenderest sympathy and encouragement. The flowers, which were in baskets, were placed on the lawn and were photographed before being taken into the house. Two large bouquets came from the First Signal corps, and some of the friends of the Milburns sent other baskets." – Marshall Everett, *Complete life of William McKinley and story of his assassination. An authentic and official memorial edition, containing every incident in the career of the immortal statesman, soldier, orator and patriot*

Although the exposition hospital had an operating theatre, it had no place for the patient to recover, so once they thought it was safe, McKinley's doctors loaded the president back into the ambulance and had him driven, very carefully, to Milburn's home. There, they placed him in a comfortable bed and then contacted his wife, who seemed to process the news stoically, though she could not bring herself to write that her husband had been shot by an anarchist. She jotted down in her diary, "Went to Niagra [sic] Falls this morning. My Dearest was receiving in a public hall on our return, when he was shot by a ...."

Around the same time, the public was informed after a bulletin was sent out by the doctors concerning McKinley's condition. Keim noted, "At 7:15 P.M. the President was returned to the electric ambulance assisted by the same willing hands and in about the same order and slowly conveyed by way of the Lincoln Park gate to the Milburn house. As the sad procession was about to leave the grounds, the evening illumination all over the building and grounds began to appear slowly at first, but in about thirty seconds and before they were turned on full head, however, the lights were turned off, leaving the exposition in utter darkness. A very appropriate mark of respect. This was very remarkable for it happened just about the Lincoln gate. As others were leaving the hospital, I was tendered a seat in the carriage of Mr. Goodrich, one of the directors of the exposition who had with him his daughter, and later we were found by Dr. Mynter. We reached the residence immediately after Dr. Rixey and the nurses, having passed the ambulance just outside of the Lincoln gate. The President was very quickly and quietly borne into the mansion and up the stairway to the apartment which had been prepared for him. Just before the party reached the Milburn house steps some hesitancy was apparent which end should go up first. Dr. Mann said the head last so it was done. I soon saw that height was needed at the rear or head so assisted them on up the winding stairs around a dangerous turn to the rear bed room where the President was carefully placed in bed. The stretcher as it was removed from the patient showed clearly the blood stains from the operation, having been used from the first till this moment. In about five minutes all the arrangements had been carried out and the President was resting comfortably as could be expected. I assisted in arranging some furniture that was crowding the room and at the same time cleared the windows so that more air could enter."

   Finally, all was in place and there was nothing more to be done that night, certainly not by any non-medical personnel, so most of the bystanders prepared to leave. In fact, due to her own delicate health, Ida McKinley was allowed to sit with her husband by his bedside for only a short period each day. Keim concluded his narrative by recording the last time he saw the president: "I was the last to leave the room, Dr. Mann leaving but a few moments before. The two hospital nurses were in the room when we entered and were most attentive, and together with myself were the only persons there when Dr. Rixey reappeared and for the first time seemed to take charge. The President, but a few moments before, seemed to be coming out from under the influence of ether and was moaning continually, evidently being in much pain. He talked and said many broken words which seemed to connect with those expressed by him before going under the influence of the ether. The surgeons, ambulance corps and friends who had assisted through these trying scenes now departed one by one, leaving Secretary Cortelyou, the medical staff, the stewards and stenographers from the White House who were there to care for the nation's sufferer. This was, I judge, about 8 o'clock. The quiet, sad but cool evening I shall never forget. I bade Mr. Cortelyou goodnight having asked him if there was anything more I could do. I was the last of the assistants to leave and regretted that I could do nothing more for the President we all loved so much."

After the surgery, McKinley spent hour after hour in bed drifting in and out of consciousness, but the doctors believed he was making progress. Indeed, the third day after his operation, McKinley was alert enough to talk, and he immediately asked about Ida's health. Things looked so promising that Vice President Theodore Roosevelt was assured that he need not cancel his planned hunting trip, so he left for Adirondack Mountains. Dr. McBurney observed, "The fact that there is no unfavorable symptom is a most favorable sign. What we are all waiting for is the lapse of time without the occurrence of inflammation or septic conditions. I want to say right here that in my opinion everything has been done for him that could and should have been done. The case has been most handsomely handled. If he lives he will owe his life to the promptness and skill of the physicians here. The question of time is of the greatest importance in case of this kind. An operation could not have been performed too soon. It was performed in one of the quickest times on record. It will be famous in the history of surgery."

Roosevelt

By Tuesday, September 10, doctors began to discuss when McKinley would be able to take some simple nourishment. In the days before intravenous feedings, it was imperative that a recovering patient eat and drink something to avoid dying of malnutrition or dehydration.

That same night, the doctors in charge of caring for McKinley issued a longer than usual bulletin assuring the public of his continuing improvement: "The condition of the President is unchanged in all important particulars His temperature is 100.6, pulse 114, respiration 28. When the operation was done on Friday last it was noted that the bullet had carried with it a short distance beneath the skin a fragment of the President s coat. This foreign material was, of course, removed, but a slight irritation of the tissues was produced, the evidence of which has appeared only to-night. It has been necessary on account of this slight disturbance to remove a few stitches and partially open the skin wound. This incident cannot give rise to other complications, but it is communicated to the public, as the surgeons in attendance wish to make their bulletins entirely frank. In consequence of this separation of the edges of the surface wound the healing of the same will be somewhat delayed. The President is now well enough to begin to take nourishment by the mouth in the form of pure beef juice."

On Wednesday, September 11, McKinley was allowed his first non-family visitors. Not only did he speak briefly with a number of Congressional representatives, he also continued to keep the broth he was given down.

A picture of Senator Hanna arriving at the Milburn house to visit McKinley

However, on Thursday, McKinley took a sudden turn for the worse; his heart was beating too fast and unevenly, owing perhaps to the strain placed on his system by having to digest the broth. After rallying briefly, his heart began to slow, and word was sent to family members and others close to McKinley that they should come to Buffalo as quickly as possible. Vice President Roosevelt was also informed of McKinley's condition and advised to head to Buffalo.

At about 2:00 a.m. on Friday morning, September 13, McKinley's heart slowed to a dangerous level, so doctors injected him with a number of drugs in the hopes of strengthening it. Again, McKinley rallied, but this time only slightly. In fact, the gangrene that had begun to form in his abdomen within seconds of the shooting had taken full hold of him and he was beginning to experience massive organ failure.

By Friday evening, it was apparent that McKinley was dying, and he told the doctors, "It is useless, gentlemen. I think we ought to have prayer." Later, he told his sobbing wife, "We are all going, we are all going. God's will be done, not ours." The couple then shared a final moment softly singing McKinley's favorite hymn, "Nearer, My God, to Thee." At 8:30 p.m., the doctors issued the following statement: "The President's condition this evening is not quite so good. His food has not agreed with him and has been stopped. Excretion has not yet been properly established. The kidneys are acting well. His pulse is not satisfactory, but has improved in the last two hours. The wound is doing well. He is resting quietly. Temperature, 100.2; pulse, 128."

Less than 6 hours later, McKinley died at 2:15 a.m. on

Saturday, September 14, 1901.

Chapter 5: No Explanation of the Deed

"Czolgosz had been carried into a side room at the northwest corner of the Temple. There he was searched, but nothing was found upon him except a letter relating to lodging. The officers washed the blood from his face and asked him who he was and why he had tried to kill the President. He made no answer at first, but finally gave the name of Nieman. He offered no explanation of the deed except that he was an Anarchist and had done his duty. A detail of exposition guards was sent for a company of soldiers. A carriage was summoned. South of the Temple a space had been roped off. The crowd tore out the iron stanchion holding the ropes and carried the ropes to the flagpole standing near by on the esplanade. 'Lynch him,' cried a hundred voices, and a start was made for one of the entrances of the Temple. Soldiers and police beat back the crowd. Guards find people were wrangling, shouting and fighting. In this confusion, Czolgosz, still bleeding, his clothes torn, and scarcely able to walk, was led out by Captain James F. Vallaly, chief of the exposition detectives; Commandant Robinson, and a squad of secret service men. Czolgosz was thrown into a carriage and three detectives jumped in with him. Captain Vallaly jumped on the driver's seat and lashed the horses into a gallop." – Marshall Everett, *Complete life of William*

McKinley and story of his assassination. An authentic and official memorial edition, containing every incident in the career of the immortal statesman, soldier, orator and patriot

McKinley's funeral train in Buffalo

In one of the greatest ironies of American history, President McKinley was assassinated just six months after Teddy Roosevelt had become Vice President, which was the result of machinations by people who wanted to remove Roosevelt from power in New York. Instead, Roosevelt succeeded McKinley, so instead of being consigned into a political abyss, Roosevelt was now the most powerful person in the United States.

In the wake of McKinley's death, Roosevelt informed the American people of what had happened and announced when McKinley's funeral would be held: "A terrible bereavement has befallen our people. The President of the United States has been struck down; a crime not only against the Chief Magistrate, but against every law-abiding and liberty-loving citizen. President McKinley crowned a life of largest love for his fellow men, of earnest endeavor for their welfare, by a death of Christian fortitude; and both the way in which he lived his life and the way in which, in the supreme hour of trial, he met his death will remain forever a precious heritage of our people. It is meet that we as a nation express our abiding love and reverence for his life, our deep sorrow for his untimely death. Now, Therefore, I, Theodore Roosevelt, President of the United States of America, do appoint Thursday next, September 19, the day in which the body of the dead President will be laid in its last earthly resting place, as a day of mourning and prayer throughout the United States. I earnestly recommend all the people to assemble on that day in their respective places of divine worship, there to bow down in submission to the will of Almighty God, and to pay out of full hearts the homage of love and reverence to the memory of the great and good President, whose death has so sorely smitten the nation."

Pictures of McKinley's state funeral back in Washington

All the while, as people focused their attention on the wounded president, the police and Secret Service had other concerns. They hauled Czolgosz to a local jail for questioning but did not have any difficulty getting a confession from him. When he was asked why he wanted to kill the president, he apparently replied, "I am an Anarchist. I am a disciple of Emma Goldman. Her words set me on fire. I deny that I have had an accomplice at any time. I don t regret my act, because I was doing what I could for the great cause. I am not connected with the Paterson group or with those Anarchists who sent Bresci to Italy to kill Humbert. I had no confidants; no one to help me. I was alone absolutely." Before the day was over, he had written and signed a statement declaring, "I was born in Detroit nearly twenty-nine years ago. My parents were Russian Poles. They came here forty-two years ago. I got my education in the public schools of Detroit and then went to Cleveland, where I got work. In Cleveland I read books on socialism and met a great many Socialists. I was pretty well known as a Socialist in the West. After being in Cleveland for several years I went to Chicago, where I remained seven months, after which I went to Newburg, on the outskirt of Cleveland, and went to work in the Newburg wire mills. During the last five years I have had as friends Anarchists in Chicago, Cleveland, Detroit, and other Western cities, and I suppose I became more or less bitter. Yes, I know I was bitter. I never had much luck at anything and this preyed upon me. It made me morose and envious, but what started the craze to kill was a lecture I heard some little time ago by Emma Goldman. She was in Cleveland and I and other Anarchists went to hear her. She set me on fire. Her doctrine that all rulers should be exterminated was what set me to thinking so that my head nearly split with the pain. Miss Goldman's words went right through me and when I left the lecture I had made up my mind that I would have to do something heroic for the cause I loved."

Goldman

Czolgosz in jail

   For his part, Czolgosz claimed that while Goldman's words were inspiration, he had planned the assassination by September 3. In fact, some believe that he had considered acting earlier by following McKinley when he took walks near his home in Canton, Ohio, but either way, the assassin admitted to police, "Eight days ago, while I was in Chicago, I read in a Chicago newspaper of President McKinley's visit to the Pan-American Exposition at Buffalo. That day I bought a ticket for Buffalo and got there with the determination to do something, but I did not know just what. I thought of shooting the President, but I had not formed a plan. I went to live at 1078 Broadway, which is a saloon and hotel. John Nowak, a Pole, a sort of politician who has led his people here for years, owns it. I told Nowak that I came to see the fair. He knew nothing about what was setting me crazy. I went to the Exposition grounds a couple of times a day. Not until Tuesday morning did the resolution to shoot the President take a hold of me. It was in my heart; there was no escape for me. I could not have conquered it had my life been at stake. There were thousands of people in town on Tuesday. I heard it was President's Day. All these people seemed bowing to the great ruler. I made up my mind to kill that ruler. I bought a 32-caliber revolver and loaded it."

The twists and turns of history can be strange, and for whatever reason, fate intervened and Czolgosz did not shoot McKinley on that Tuesday. Instead, as he explained, "On Tuesday night I went to the Fair grounds and was near the railroad gate when the Presidential party arrived. I tried to get near him, but the police forced me back. They forced everybody back so that the great ruler could pass. I was close to the President when he got into the grounds, but was afraid to attempt the assassination because there were so many men in the bodyguard that watched him. I was not afraid of them or that I should get hurt, but afraid I might be seized and that my chance would be gone forever. Well, he went away that time and I went home. On Wednesday I went to the grounds and stood right near the President, right under him near the stand from which he spoke. I thought half a dozen times of shooting while he was speaking, but I could not get close enough. I was afraid I might miss, and then the great crowd was always jostling, and I was afraid lest my aim fail. I waited on Wednesday, and the President got into his carriage again, and a lot of men were about him and formed a cordon that I could not get through. I was tossed about by the crowd, and my spirits were getting pretty low. I was almost hopeless that night as I went home."

Had Czolgosz's missed opportunities changed his mind, there's no telling how differently things may have gone for the nation, but he remained determined. "Yesterday morning I went again to the Exposition grounds. Emma Goldman's speech was still burning me up. I waited near the central entrance for the President, who was to board his special train from that gate, but the police allowed nobody but the President's party to pass where the train waited, so I stayed at the grounds all day waiting. During yesterday I first thought of hiding my pistol under my handkerchief. I was afraid if I had to draw, it from my pocket I would be seen and seized by the guards. I got to the Temple of Music the first one and waited at the spot where the reception was to be held. Then he came, the President the ruler and I got in line and trembled and trembled until I got right up to him, and then I shot him twice, through my white handkerchief. I would have fired more, but I was stunned by a blow in the face a frightful blow that knocked me down and then everybody jumped on me. I thought I would be killed and was surprised the way they treated me."

Czolgosz's decision to murder McKinley is truly ironic considering that just a few days earlier, *The Free Society Newspaper* accused him of being an anti-anarchist spy. It seems that in his enthusiasm, he had been asking too many questions about what anarchism was, where one could find a meeting of anarchists, and who the local leaders were. The *Free Society* had warned, "ATTENTION! The attention of the comrades is called to another spy. He is well dressed, of medium height, rather narrow shoulders, blond and about 25 years of age. Up to the present he has made his appearance in Chicago and Cleveland. In the former place he remained but a short time, while in Cleveland he disappeared when the comrades had confirmed themselves of his identity and were on the point of exposing him. His demeanor is of the usual sort, pretending to be greatly interested in the cause, asking for names or soliciting aid for acts of contemplated violence. If this same individual makes his appearance elsewhere the comrades are warned in advance, and can act accordingly."

Chapter 6: An Anarchist!

"Within a few minutes after the shooting of President McKinley at Buffalo, and before anything was known of the identity of the assailant, news of the affair was in every American town and village to which the telegraph reaches. Probably in every town those to whom this first report came exclaimed: 'An Anarchist!' and many thousands added bitter denunciation of all anarchists. When later news arrived it was established definitely by the confession of the would-be slayer that he was an anarchist and fired the shots in a desire to further the cause of those who believe as he does. What, then, is anarchism, and who are the anarchists that the destruction of the head of a republican government can further their cause? … According to Zenker, himself an anarchistic theorist, anarchism means, in its ideal sense, 'the perfect, unfettered self-government of the individual, and consequently the absence of any kind of external government.' That such a state is possible not one of the anarchistic philosophers has contended, and each has been eager to hold up his neighbor's plan, if not also his own, as a Utopia. Its realization, said Protidhon, pioneer of the cult, would be an entirely new world, a new Eden, a land of the perfect idealization of freedom and of equality." –

Marshall Everett, *Complete life of William McKinley and story of his assassination. An authentic and official memorial edition, containing every incident in the career of the immortal statesman, soldier, orator and patriot*

   Born in Russia in the late 19th century, Emma Goldman had come to the United States as a teen and quickly grew attracted to anarchy and socialism over what she viewed as unfair class structures in her new home, especially in the wake of the Haymarket riots. But while many simply grumbled about the Gilded Age in private or denounced it in print, Goldman was a woman of action, from being involved in the attempted assassination of tycoon Henry Clay Frick to publishing anarchist journals and passing around information about contraception.

   As a result, Goldman was already notorious before McKinley's death, and when Czolgosz mentioned her by name, it had obvious ramifications for her as well. Indeed, as soon as the authorities learned that Czolgosz had been influenced in his plan by Goldman, they immediately saw an opportunity to arrest her, for they had long been concerned about her anti-American activities and were looking for an excuse to take her into custody. Of course, it did not help that she had spoken out about the case and told a reporter, "The boy in Buffalo is a creature at bay. Millions of people are ready to spring on him and tear him limb from limb. He committed the act for no personal reasons or gain. He did it for what is his ideal: the good of the people. That is why my sympathies are with him. On the other hand, William McKinley, suffering and probably near death, is merely a human being to me now. That is why I would nurse him."

Goldman remembered the moment she learned she had been named by Czolgosz: "I went to the stationery store to see the owner. … While I was waiting for the man to fill out his order, I caught the headline of the newspaper lying on his desk: 'ASSASSIN OF PRESIDENT MCKINLEY AN ANARCHIST, CONFESSES TO HAVING BEEN INCITED BY EMMA GOLDMAN, WOMAN ANARCHIST WANTED.' By great effort I strove to preserve my composure, completed the business, and walked out of the store. At the next corner I bought several papers and went to a restaurant to read them. They were filled with the details of the tragedy, reporting also the police raid of the Isaak house in Chicago and the arrest of everyone found there. The authorities were going to hold the prisoners until Emma Goldman was found, the papers stated. Already two hundred detectives had been sent out throughout the country to track down Emma Goldman. … When I was through with the papers, it became clear to me that I must immediately go to Chicago. The Isaak family, Hippolyte, our old comrade Jay Fox, a most active man in the labour movement, and a number of others were being held without bail until I should be found. It was plainly my duty to surrender myself. I knew there was neither reason nor the least proof to connect me with the shooting. I would go to Chicago."

Once in Chicago, Goldman was indeed arrested and interrogated, but there was no evidence to convict her of anything not covered by her right to free speech, so she was released. Undeterred, she shocked and horrified even her most ardent supporters by publicly defending Czolgosz: "As an anarchist, I am opposed to violence. But if the people want to do away with assassins, they must do away with the conditions which produce murderers."

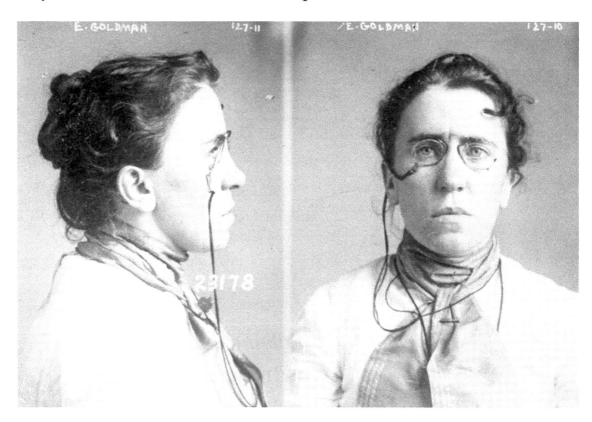

Goldman's 1901 mug shot

EMMA GOLDMAN, HIGH PRIESTESS OF ANARCHY, WHOSE SPEECHES INSPIRED CZOLGOSZ TO HIS CRIME.

EMMA GOLDMAN

SPEECH THAT PROMPTED MURDEROUS ASSAULT ON THE PRESIDENT.

The *Chicago Daily Tribune*'s condemnation of Goldman

This stance proved to be very harmful not just to Goldman but to the entire movement, and it brought down the wrath of many across the grieving nation. The new president, Teddy Roosevelt, himself something of a populist, declared, "The anarchist, and especially the anarchist in the United States, is merely one type of criminal, more dangerous than any other because he represents the same depravity in a greater degree. The man who advocates anarchy directly or indirectly, in any shape or fashion, or the man who apologizes for anarchists and their deeds, makes himself morally accessory to murder before the fact. The anarchist is a criminal whose perverted instincts lead him to prefer confusion and chaos to the most beneficent form of social order. His protest of concern for workingmen is outrageous in its impudent falsity; for if the political institutions of this country do not afford opportunity to every honest and intelligent son of toil, then the door of hope is forever closed against him. The anarchist is everywhere not merely the enemy of system and of progress, but the deadly foe of liberty. If ever anarchy is triumphant, its triumph will last for but one red moment, to be succeeded, for ages by the gloomy night of despotism."

As Goldman herself noted, "After the death of McKinley the campaign against anarchism and its adherents continued with increased venom. The press, the pulpit, and other public mouthpieces were frantically vying with each other in their fury against the common enemy. … Anti-anarchist bills followed each other in quick succession, their congressional sponsors busy inventing new methods for the extermination of anarchists. Senator Hawley evidently did not consider his professional wisdom sufficient to slay the anarchist dragon. He declared publicly that he would give a thousand dollars to get a shot at an anarchist. It was a cheap offer considering the price Czolgosz had paid for his shot."

On September 13, as McKinley lay dying, Czolgosz was transferred from the police headquarters where he had been held since the shooting to the Erie County Women's Penitentiary. While he was there, he was apparently a model prisoner, cooperative and pleasant to the guards, whom he seemed to view not as his captors but as fellow victims of the system of government under which Americans were laboring.

Three days later, he was brought before County Judge Emery for arraignment. After the Grand Jury indicted him for murder, he was transferred to Auburn State Prison. The indictment read, in part:

"That the said Leon F. Czolgosz, … with force and arms in and upon one William McKinley…being, willfully, feloniously and from a deliberate and premeditated design to effect the death of said William McKinley, did make an assault, and the said Leon F. Czolgosz, alias Fred Nieman, then and there willfully, feloniously and from a deliberate and premeditated design to effect the death of the said William McKinley, did shoot off and discharge to, at, against and upon the said William McKinley a certain pistol and firearm, then and there charged and loaded with gunpowder and leaden bullets, …shot out of the pistol and firearm…in and upon the stomach, abdomen and body of the said William McKinley, one mortal wound…the said William McKinley…until the fourteenth day of September…did languish, and, languishing, did live, on which said last-mentioned day he…of the said mortal wound, did die; contrary to the form of the statute in such case made and provided, and against the peace of the people of the State of New York and their dignity.

(Signed.) THOMAS PENNEY, District Attorney of Erie County."

Apparently, Neiman was an Americanized version of his mother's maiden name, and he sometimes used the alias Fred Nieman when he was trying to hide what he was doing.

Fittingly, the arraignment itself proved to be something a mystery to many people, as Czolgosz refused to speak out on his own behalf or even allow his lawyers to do so. Meanwhile, Everett gave a moving description of the event:

> "'Are you guilty, or not guilty?' was the question which the Law asked of him.
>
> He was placed with hands unbound in the presence of a sedate tribunal of one of the tribunals which all the organs of his reed had been maligning in their every issue; and there he was asked:
>
> 'Are you guilty, or not guilty?'
>
> District Attorney Penney almost shouted the words at Leon Czolgosz, sitting in the county courtroom at 3 o clock this afternoon. The assassin did not even turn his eyes toward his questioner.
>
> 'Are you guilty? Answer yes or no!' thundered the district attorney, but the fair-haired monster in the chair paid no heed.
>
> 'Do you understand what has been read?' asked

Mr. Penney.

…The assassin leaned forward in his chair, then dropped his eyes, then leaned back in silence.

'You have been indicted for murder in the first degree,' said Mr. Penney.

…Judge Loren L. Lewis, former justice of the Supreme Court, who had been assigned to the defense of the assassin by Judge Edward K. Emery, then arose and addressed the court. It was at once apparent that the duty was distasteful, but Mr. Lewis entered a plea of 'Not Guilty.'"

After he entered the plea, Lewis went on to explain to the court his awkward situation; while Czolgosz would happily speak with all those around him, he would have nothing to do with his court-appointed attorneys. Everett noted, "Attorney Lewis then told the court that he had called upon the prisoner, but had been met with a stubborn refusal to discuss the case. Czolgosz would not even admit that he wished the services of counsel. Mr. Lewis asked the court for permission to introduce alienists to examine into the prisoner's mental condition, as this step had already been taken by the attorneys for the people. He mentioned incidentally that he was sorry his name had been connected with the case, but that as a lawyer and an officer of the court he felt himself obligated to carry out its wishes. ... Mr. Lewis request to be permitted to introduce alienists gave rise to the prevalent belief that the defense will be built upon the theory of insanity."

Chapter 7: Guilty

"Leon Czolgosz was a member of several Anarchist clubs in Cleveland, one of which was named 'Sila,' which means 'force.' Trie club met at the corner of Tod street and Third avenue, over a saloon which, it is said. Czolgosz once owned. Three years before the assassination the club disbanded and he left it, but joined another. 'Czolgosz made no secret of the fact that he was an Anarchist,' said Anton Zwolinski, a Cleveland Pole. 'He was always talking about it and trying to force Anarchists principles on every one whom he talked with. He was a great coward, however, and I am surprised he had the nerve to do as he did. It would not surprise me to learn that he is merely the tool of some other persons. When the Sila Club broke up Czolgosz joined another one.' ... Czolgosz was placed on trial before Justice Truman C. White of the State Supreme Bench, at Buffalo, on Monday, September 23. On the following day the jury found him guilty, and on Thursday, September 26, he was sentenced to death by electrocution in the week beginning October 28. He refused to consult with the attorneys appointed to defend him, and practically made no defense." – Marshall Everett, *Complete life of William*

McKinley and story of his assassination. An authentic and official memorial edition, containing every incident in the career of the immortal statesman, soldier, orator and patriot

It seems likely Czolgosz shunned his attorneys because, at least to him, they represented the establishment and the government, but regardless, since he would not speak to them, his lawyers, Lewis and Judge R. C. Titus, simply went with a plea of insanity. Of course, the prosecution was able to show without a doubt that Czolgosz definitely pulled the trigger, so there could be no doubt about that. With little strategy available to him, Lewis admitted Czolgosz's guilt but insisted that "the only question that can be discussed or considered in this case is ... whether that act was that of a sane person. If it was, then the defendant is guilty of the murder ... If it was the act of an insane man, then he is not guilty of murder but should be acquitted of that charge and would then be confined in a lunatic asylum."

In an article published in *The Journal of Mental Pathology* in January 1902, Dr. Carlos McDonald, who had examined Czolgosz while he was in prison, observed, "In view of the great importance of the case, it is regrettable that no experts were called to testify on the trial as to the prisoner's mental condition, in order that it might appear on the record of the trial that his mental state was inquired into and determined by competent authority. Had the experts on either side been given the opportunity of thus stating officially their unanimous conclusion, together with the grounds on which it was based and the methods by which it was reached, it would have left in the public mind no room for reasonable doubt as to its absolute correctness, and that it had been arrived at only by the rules of professional conduct governing the examination of such cases."

Still, McDonald recognized that the defense was indeed doing the best it could under the parameters that Czolgosz himself had set. After all, it was very difficult to defend a man who seemed to have no desire to be acquitted. McDonald recalled, "On Thursday, September 19th, 1901, I received a telegram requesting me to meet Mr. Adelbert Moot, President of the Erie County Bar Association, in Buffalo, New York, on the following morning. On my arrival in Buffalo the next day, Mr. Moot informed me that he had sent for me for the purpose of requesting me to inquire into the mental condition of Leon F. Czolgosz…whose trial was to begin on the following Monday. Mr. Moot further stated in substance that three local experts had already examined the prisoner for the District Attorney, but in view of the enormity of the offense and the fact that there obviously could be no legitimate defense other than insanity, it was deemed important, in the interests of justice, that his mental condition should be investigated by other experts acting in behalf of the defense, or at least independently of the prosecution to the end that the prisoner should be accorded every legal right, there being no desire to convict him if he were not mentally responsible, and that I had been selected for this responsible duty."

McDonald seemed convinced that in spite of the nation's demand for swift and fierce justice, there was nothing rigged about the trial, and that the state seemed committed to giving Czolgosz as fair a trial as the circumstances allowed. He continued, "With a deep sense of the responsibility involved, I consented to act, provided it should be distinctly understood that I was not there as a partisan expert in behalf of either side, but simply in a professional capacity to aid in determining the real mental state of the prisoner, and providing further that my selection would be acceptable to the eminent counsel whom the Bar Association had selected for the defense, should they decide to accept that duty, a matter which was then undecided. On the following morning — Saturday — Mr. Moot informed me that the gentlemen referred to had consented to act…. They also assented readily to my proposal to invite Dr. Arthur W. Hurd to become associated with me professionally in the case…. Being unable to establish communication with Dr. Hurd before evening of that day, and in view of the short time intervening before the trial, I decided to make a preliminary examination of Czolgosz alone, and did so that afternoon, in the District Attorney's office, first disclosing to him my identity and the object of my interview, and informing him of his legal right to decline to answer any question I might ask him."

   McDonald ultimately concluded that the defense's basis for its insanity plea was pretty weak. "I examined him again on the following day — Sunday — in the jail, jointly with Dr. Hurd, and in the presence of one of his guards who was questioned at length, respecting his observations of him in the jail, as to his habits of eating, sleeping, talking, reading, etc. We subsequently interviewed the District Attorney and the Superintendent of Police, General Bull, who gave us all the facts and information in their possession respecting the case. The statement which Czolgosz made to the District Attorney shortly after his arrest, throws much light on his mental condition on the day of the crime, but that official deemed it his duty to refuse to allow me to publish it. We also conferred at length with the people's experts — Drs. Fowler, Crego and Putnam, who stated to us separately and in detail their observations and examinations of him. We also observed him carefully in the court room throughout the trial. After our examination of Czolgosz, on Sunday, we reached the conclusion, independently of each other, that he was sane, and we so informed his counsel, on Monday morning before the trial began. It should be said that owing to the limited time — two days — at our disposal prior to the trial and the fact that his family relatives resided in a distant state and were not accessible for interrogation, we were unable to obtain a history of his heredity, beyond what he himself gave us."

On the other hand, the prosecutor was able to make much of Czolgosz's obsession with anarchism and paint him as a man who knew perfectly well what he was doing and what the consequences were likely to be when he killed the president. Then, to top everything off, White sent the jury off with pretty clear instructions to ignore any claims that Czolgosz was mentally unbalanced. According to McDonald, "The jury retired for deliberation about 4 p. m., and returned in less than half an hour with a verdict of guilty of murder in the first degree. Czolgosz heard the verdict of the jury standing, and without appreciable display of emotion. Several of the jurors were reported to have said after the trial, that the jury was in favor of conviction unanimously from the first, and could have rendered a verdict without leaving their seats, but deemed it best to make a pretense at deliberation 'for appearance' sake.' Czolgosz was remanded to jail for two days, and on Thursday, September 26th, was sentenced to be executed by electricity at Auburn Prison, in the week beginning October 28th, 1901. When Czolgosz returned to his cell after his conviction he ate a hearty supper, and soon thereafter went to bed and slept continuously until midnight, when the guard was changed, when he awoke for a few minutes, and then slept again until 6 a. m., when he arose and took a short walk in the cell corridor, after which he made a careful toilet, and at 7.30 partook of a hearty breakfast. He talked freely, as usual, on ordinary topics, but maintained his usual silence respecting his crime, and would not talk of the trial or the verdict. On Thursday, September 26th, he was removed from the Buffalo jail to the State Prison at Auburn, N. Y., where he was confined in a 'death cell,' until his execution took place."

Chapter 8: Wiped from the World

"And behind these more or less gentle and philosophic pathfinders in anarchism have come the 'doers of the word' the redhanded assassins of history. … During all these years the anarchist leaders had openly preached violence, and had taught their followers how to make dynamite bombs. They went so far as to give in detail their plans for fighting the police and militia, and caused more or less consternation among the timid residents of the city. … Looking back upon the work of anarchy in the last fifty years or more its results should be discouraging to any but the most hair-brained [sic] of the type. Its violence has not altered or unsettled the course of a single government against which it has been directed. If individuals here and there have been murdered the crimes have reacted upon the tools of butchery, most frequently sending the assassin to a dishonored grave, leaving the name of his kinsman a reproach for all time. The seed of ideal anarchy still is being sown, however, and its crop of crimes and criminals may be expected to be harvested in the future, as in the past, unless, by some concerted, radical efforts of civilization its bloody sophistries are to be wiped from the world." – Marshall Everett, *Complete life of William McKinley and story of his assassination. An authentic and official memorial edition, containing every incident in the career of the immortal statesman, soldier, orator and patriot*

On October 29, 1901, less than two months after he shot McKinley, Czolgosz was scheduled to be executed at Auburn Prison. This was swift justice even by the standards of that era, but he put up no resistance and made no legal appeals. Charles Huntley witnessed the execution and subsequently described it: "Czolgosz did not show any signs of fear and he did not tremble or turn pale; he walked into the death room between two men, and walked with a firm step. He stumbled as he came into the room but did not fall, nor did his knees weaken. I was quite surprised at his demeanor, as was everyone else, I should say. He was perfectly strong and calm. He just slid himself into the chair exactly as a man might who expected to enjoy a half hour's repose. The fact that in a moment a death current was to be forced through him did not seem to perturb him in the least. … He spoke very plainly and in a voice which did not waver in the slightest degree. He said first that he was not sorry for having killed the President, and, as the straps which bound his jaws were put in place, he said that he was sorry he could not see his father. … It was a general surprise to hear his voice after the men had begun to affix the electrodes. The witnesses were somewhat startled and were amazed at the man's calmness. We all kept our eyes on him and listened most attentively. But the men at work beside him and in front, of him did not pause. They kept on affixing the appliances. Evidently Czolgosz had prepared something to say and what he said was part of his prepared piece. … I wouldn't say that he tried to make a hero of himself. There was no spirit of bravado manifest at all. He said a few things just as if he felt it his duty to say them."

Apparently Czolgosz's last words were, "I killed the President because he was the enemy of the good people – the good working people. I am not sorry for my crime." However, some who were listening thought that, at the very last minute, he said softly, as if fighting his emotion,

"I am only sorry I could not get to see my father."

  Sheriff Samuel Caldwell, who was present at the execution, reported, "I was impressed with the idea that the assassin was a man of great nerve. Although guards had hold of his arms, the prisoner could have walked unaided to the chair. Aside from the prisoner's last words, there was not a sound in the death chamber, and the prisoner himself gave no evidence of fear. As soon as he had been seated in the chair and his face covered so that his nose and mouth were alone exposed, Warden Mead raised his hand and Electrician Davis turned on the current which snuffed out the prisoner's life as with a snap of the finger. The electrician then felt the prisoner's jugular vein. Dr. MacDonald did the same, and was followed by Prison Physician Gerin. The doctors then stepped back, and Warden Mead again raised his hand. Again the current was applied and was continued about 50 seconds. When the electricity was again shut off, the physicians examined the body by the usual means, and at the end pronounced that the man was dead. The witnesses left the death chamber before the body was removed to the operating table in the autopsy room. I signed the document. swearing that I saw the electrocution of the assassin. The doctors remained for the autopsy, but I came home immediately. The prisoner's nerve was evidenced by his conduct from the moment he entered the death chamber.

No groan escaped him, and his lips did not even move except when he was making his final statement to the effect that he did not repent his crime. When the electricity entered the assassin's body it stiffened with successive jerks, but death was so quick that he did not have time to groan."

In keeping with the practice of the day, Czolgosz was given three jolts of 1800 volts each, and the physicians on hand pronounced him dead at 7:14. His brother, Waldek, and his brother-in-law, Frank Bandowski, were present to witness the execution and afterward approached the warden and asked to have Czolgosz's body to take home for burial. However, the warden would not allow it and told them they "would never be able to take it away" without being mobbed by the crowds gathered outside. Instead, Czolgosz's body was taken back into custody and turned over to Edward Spitzka for autopsy.

DR. EDWARD ANTHONY SPITZKA
Director and Professor of General Anatomy
The Daniel Bangle Institute of Anatomy of
the Jefferson Medical College
Philadelphia, Pa.

Spitzka

In answering some of the lingering questions concerning Czolgosz's mental state, Spitzka could only say, "It is a probable fact that certain classical aberrations from the normal standard of brain structure are commonly encountered in some criminals and degraded classes of society; and some workers who have attempted to found a school of degeneracy have endeavored to explain the manifestation of crime and other psychic abnormalities by the fact of 'accidental persistence of lower types of human organization.' But these structural anomalies, so far as they have been described in the brains of criminals, are too few and too insufficiently corroborated to warrant us in drawing conclusions from them. Various perversions or anomalies of mind may exist in this class without presenting a uniform criminal type from the anatomical aspect. Of course, it is far more difficult, — and it is impossible in some cases — to establish sanity upon the results of an examination of the brain, than it is to prove insanity. This difficulty is so much the more complex because some forms of psychoses have absolutely no ascertainable anatomical basis. The assumption has been made that these psychoses depend rather on circulatory and bio-chemical disturbances. So far as this question touches upon the brain and body of Czolgosz, there have been found absolutely none of those conditions of any of the viscera that could have been at the bottom of any mental derangement. Taking all in all, the verdict must be, 'socially diseased and perverted, but not mentally diseased.' The most horrible violations of human law cannot always be condoned by the plea of insanity. 'The wild beast slumbers in us all. It is not always necessary to invoke insanity to explain its awakening.'"

Following the autopsy, Czolgosz's body was buried in the prison cemetery, with acid having been doused on it to speed up decomposition. Most of his belongings were burned, but the gun he used in his heinous act was kept and is now part of collection of the Buffalo History Museum.

Though he would obviously not live to see it or comprehend it, Czolgosz's assassination of McKinley may have had a bigger impact on history than any other president's assassin other than John Wilkes Booth. Even without diving into his life and career, the fact that Theodore Roosevelt is on Mount Rushmore alongside George Washington, Thomas Jefferson, and Abraham Lincoln says volumes about his place in American history. That alone makes clear Roosevelt is among the nation's most influential and important Presidents.

Thanks to the death of McKinley, Roosevelt had the opportunity to mold the presidency in crucial ways. Roosevelt was able to create the "bully pulpit" of the presidency and ensure that he set the nation's legislative agenda by giving press statements regularly. Every president has since used the office to attempt to determine the nation's legislative priorities.
This personal strengthening of the presidency spilled

over into an administrative augmentation of the office of President. Though the Sherman Anti Trust Act had been passed in the 1880s, all presidents before Roosevelt underutilized its power. Roosevelt consolidated much of the power delegated to him by Congress and ensured that the President took an active role in administering the government of the United States. He also expanded the Presidential cabinet and created many new administrative departments, widening the breadth of the nation's federal bureaucracy. Only his fifth cousin, Franklin, would outshine him in this pursuit decades later.

On domestic policy, Theodore Roosevelt's presidency was the height of American progressivism, again outshone only by his distant cousin decades later. Roosevelt brought the ideology of limited, free-market government to its heels and instituted numerous reforms geared towards breaking corporate power and aiding consumers.

Roosevelt's presidency is also credited with making America a global player in international relations. The Panama Canal and the Roosevelt Corollary ensured the U.S. would dominate the Western Hemisphere, and the Portsmouth Treaty also expanded the nation's influence in places it had previously never gone. Roosevelt's expansion of the military and support for an interventionist policy was a marked departure from previous administrations; until Roosevelt, the United

States had been rigidly isolationist since Washington offered his neutrality advice as President.

Thus, it was Roosevelt who ensured the nation would not merely be an economic powerhouse but also participate actively and powerfully in the international sphere. It can safely be said that Roosevelt opened the doors to what would become the "American Century."

The Kennedy Assassination

John and Jackie Kennedy arriving in Dallas the morning of November 22, 1963

Chapter 1: Before Dallas

A Camelot Sized Mirage

In many ways, John Fitzgerald Kennedy and his young family were the perfect embodiment of the '60s. The decade began with a sense of idealism, personified by the attractive Kennedy, his beautiful and fashionable wife Jackie, and his young children. Months into his presidency, Kennedy exhorted the country to reach for the stars, calling upon the nation to send a man to the Moon and back by the end of the decade. In 1961, Kennedy made it seem like anything was possible, and Americans were eager to believe him. The Kennedy years would be fondly and famously labeled "Camelot" during an interview given by the recently widowed Jackie Kennedy shortly after her husband's assassination, suggesting an almost mythical quality about the young President and his family. Much of the glamor and vigor of Camelot, if not the majority of it, was supplied by the former First Lady, whose elegance and grace made her the most popular woman in the world. Her popularity threatened to eclipse even her husband's, who famously quipped on one Presidential trip to France that he was "the man who accompanied Jacqueline Kennedy to Paris."

As it turned out, the decade would reflect both the glossy and idealistic portrayal of John F. Kennedy, as well as the uglier truths of the man and his administration. The country would achieve Kennedy's goal of a manned moon mission, and the landmark Civil Rights Act of 1964 finally guaranteed minorities their civil rights and restored equality, ensuring that the country "would live out the true meaning of its creed." But the idealism and optimism of the decade was quickly shattered by the President's own assassination. The rest of the decade would be marred by the Vietnam War, and by the time Robert F. Kennedy and Martin Luther King, Jr. were assassinated in 1968, the country was irreversibly jaded.

It was only natural that the mythology surrounding the President and his administration would bloom in the wake of his tragic death, but it has also obscured the political realities of 1963 and the reason John F. Kennedy was even in Dallas on that fateful day.

The Election of 1960

Kennedy's assassination has frozen him in time as the image of a youthful President seemingly capable of anything, but his election in 1960 and the first few years of his presidency had been a political dogfight.

At the start of the campaigning for the Democratic Party's nomination, a poll of Congressional Democrats ranked Senate Majority Leader Lyndon B. Johnson at the top for the nomination, followed by Adlai Stevenson, Stuart Symington, and John F. Kennedy. Back in 1960 it was conceivable that a candidate could skip the primaries entirely and then rely on the party establishment at the convention to make them the nominee. Senator Johnson thought the primaries were risky business, since losing one would signal that a candidate was not viable among voters and extinguish any hope of winning the nomination, and he felt he didn't need to take this risk. Senator Kennedy, on the other hand, thought a victory in the primaries would make it hard for delegates to deny the nomination to that candidate. Privately, John and his father Joe had discussed the 1960 Presidential Election since Kennedy's Vice-Presidential hopes in 1956. John thought his Catholicism was the biggest barrier to the Presidency, while his father thought otherwise. To Joseph Sr., the nation had grown beyond its anti-Catholic sentiments and was ready to accept a Catholic President. Furthermore, since the 1956 Convention, the media had viewed Senator Kennedy as the frontrunner for the Democratic nomination. Polls of Democratic voters confirmed this view, showing Senator Kennedy in a tie with former nominee Adlai Stevenson for the 1960 nomination.

As Kennedy's campaign anticipated, the candidate succeeded in the primaries that Johnson chose to abstain from. Throughout the few primaries that were conducted that year, John had the opportunity to prove his broad appeal to the Convention's party elders, and his win in the largely white and Protestant state of West Virginia seemed to amply prove his claim that he did not just appeal narrowly to fellow Catholics. This gave the convention little reason to deny Kennedy the nomination, and he was thus chosen over Johnson to be the Democratic candidate for President of the United States.

John preferred Lyndon Johnson as vice President for several political reasons. Electorally, he thought Johnson made sense: being from Texas, he could help balance Kennedy's decidedly New England-centric appeal. Additionally, Johnson was much older than the youthful Kennedy, which would help deflect concerns about the candidate's age and inexperience. And in the realm of governing, Johnson was a veteran in Washington, having risen to the position of Senate Majority Leader and becoming one of the most powerful wielders of power in the history of that body. Johnson's experience would prove critical in governing the nation, as he had the connections and know-how that John Kennedy admittedly did not. Moreover, much as LBJ had tried to balance the differences in his party over Civil Rights, Kennedy was worried the issue would break his chances of winning the general election. Picking a Southerner like Johnson allowed him to allay the concerns of Dixiecrats and Southern Democrats.

John's brother Bobby, however, was not convinced that Johnson was a good selection. Candidly, Bobby thought Johnson was an intellectual lightweight, an accusation that was not only way off the mark but also clearly tinged with sectionalist prejudices. Bobby, from Massachusetts, thought the Texas Senator was wholly unintelligent. When John called Johnson to ask him to be the Vice Presidential nominee, Bobby reportedly contacted Johnson to ask that he decline the offer. This accusation has never been confirmed; however, it is known that Johnson contacted John again to confirm that he had actually been offered the nomination. Upon hearing it straight from the horse's mouth, he accepted the Vice Presidential nomination.

In the general election, Kennedy and Johnson faced Vice President Richard Nixon and Former Senator Henry Cabot Lodge, who John had defeated for the Senate seat in Massachusetts 8 years earlier. To open the campaign, Kennedy gave his famous New Frontier Speech at the Democratic Convention. In it, he branded his forward-looking ambitions for the United States. Johnson's role in the campaign proved to be exactly what Kennedy intended. The Vice Presidential candidate campaigned diligently throughout the South, especially in his native Texas, which held a significant chunk of electoral votes that would be critical on Election Day. At the same time, the state was not part of the "Solid South," and was something of a swing state: it voted for Truman and Eisenhower in the three preceding elections.

By November, the gap between the two candidates was

paper thin. Kennedy remained strong among "white ethnics," labor and African-Americans, while Nixon appealed to rural Protestants, the West Coast, and parts of the South. On Election Day, the popular vote was as close as polls suggested: Kennedy won by a hair, with 49.7% to Nixon's 49.5%. The Electoral College vote, however, was a different story, with Kennedy winning with 303 votes to Nixon's 219. The vote was so close that many still accuse Kennedy and his surrogates of fixing the election, with charges of fraud clouding matters in Texas and Illinois. Nixon would later be praised for refusing to contest the election, but in the following decades it was made clear how much his surrogates had tried to overturn the election.

Johnson's influence had proven critically significant. In some states, he proved to be the critical margin of difference. This included his home state of Texas, which the Kennedy-Johnson ticket carried by just about 2 percentage points. In other Southern states, Johnson merely ensured that the Republicans made no surprise gains. The Johnson factor was probably critical in a state like Arkansas, which the Democratic ticket won by just over 7 percentage points. The "Solid South," despite Johnson, was not as solid in 1960 as it once was: the entry of Harry Byrd as a third party candidate took up some of the South's electoral votes in Alabama and Mississippi. Without Johnson, perhaps other states would have thrown their votes to the third party candidate.

The Election of 1960 demonstrated the various potential political pitfalls that awaited the Kennedy Administration and his reelection campaign in 1964. He had barely managed to win the election in 1960, and the issues that nearly fractured his party, particularly the Civil Rights Movement, would dominate headlines in 1962 and 1963.

A Rough Start

From the very beginning, Kennedy's presidency was an eventful one. The first major crisis came in the form of the Bay of Pigs debacle. In early 1961, just months after his inauguration, Kennedy felt the need to deal with the emerging communist threat that was growing just miles off the US border. Fidel Castro had risen to power less than a decade earlier in the island country, and Castro was forming increasingly strong ties with the Soviet Union. Such an alliance challenged basic US security interests. Hoping to otherthrow the regime, Kennedy approved of a CIA-led plan to invade the country and oust the leader by igniting revolution. Unfortunately, the invasion failed, and Kennedy was left with an international embarrassment.

The failed Bay of Pigs Invasion indirectly led to the next major foreign policy crisis: the Cuban Missile Crisis. The Soviets, hoping to capitalize on a weak and seemingly incompetent US policy, began stationing nuclear missiles in Cuba. These could strike the U.S. homeland, representing an unprecedented threat to the country. For Kennedy, this was unacceptable. Attacking the sites, which represented the easiest way to rid Cuba of missiles, also posed the threat of nuclear war. Diplomacy, however, seemed a longer and more difficult route. After weeks of negotiations, with the world braced for nuclear war, the Soviets agreed to remove the missiles if the US removed its own stationed in Turkey. Nuclear war was averted.

Civil Rights Movement

At home, Kennedy came into office just as the nation was divided on the issue of race. After a 1960 Supreme Court decision in *Boynton v. Virginia*, bus segregation was made illegal on new grounds: it violated the interstate commerce clause of the Constitution, by regulating the movement of people across state lines. With this victory in hand, the Freedom Rides of 1961 began. Organized primarily by a new group – the Congress on Racial Equality (CORE) – the Freedom Rides followed the same guidance that inspired the Montgomery Boycott and the Greensboro Sit-Ins – nonviolent direct action. The purpose of the Freedom Rides was the test the Supreme Court's decision by riding from Virginia to Louisiana on integrated busses. This was notably the first major Civil Rights event that included a large segment of white participants.

Both black and white Northerners had participated in the Freedom Rides, and civil rights activists sought other ways to harness their energy and activism in the next few years. After the Freedom Rides, leaders like Medgar Evers initiated voter registration drives that could help register black voters and build community organizations that could help make their votes count. In February 1962, representatives of various civil rights groups formed the Council of Federated Organizations (COFO), and that Spring they began voter registration organizing in the Mississippi Delta, only to meet fierce resistance from authorities and white-supremacists, including arrests, beatings, shootings, arson, and murder. Similar voter registration campaigns met similar resistance in Louisiana, Alabama, Georgia, and South Carolina. Nevertheless, by 1963 the registration campaigns were widespread and just as crucial as Freedom Rides to integration.

After a drawn out lawsuit, a young man named James Meredith was finally set to attend the University of Mississippi in 1962, a college campus attended by thousands of young men each year. But James Meredith would be no typical young man at the university; he would be its only black man.

As Meredith repeatedly attempted to enter campus that September, he was prevented by a mob, which included

Mississippi Governor Ross Barnett. Governor Barnett had earlier attempted to stop Meredith's admission by changing state laws to ban anyone who had been convicted of a state crime. Meredith's "crime" had been false voter registration. An avowed segregationist, Barnett asserted, ""The Good Lord was the original segregationist. He put the black man in Africa. ...He made us white because he wanted us white, and He intended that we should stay that way." And according to Barnett, the reason so many blacks lived in Mississippi at the time was because "they love our way of life here, and that way is segregation." Barnett would later be fined $10,000 and sentenced to jail for contempt (though he never ended up going to jail or paying the fine).

On September 30, Meredith was escorted by U.S. Marshals sent in by Attorney General Bobby Kennedy only to have a white mob attack the marshals, a melee in which nearly 200 people were injured. President Kennedy had to send in the Army to allow Meredith to stay at school. Meredith would receive a bachelor's degree in political science in August 1963. He would later be shot in the back and legs during a civil rights march in 1966 by a white man attempting to assassinate him.

The Civil Rights Movement was in full throttle during the summer of 1963, reaching a crescendo with the March on Washington and Martin Luther King Jr.'s iconic "I Have A Dream" speech on the steps of the Lincoln

Memorial, but the Kennedy Administration's relatively tepid support of civil rights was dividing the Democratic Party. Southern conservatives thought Kennedy had proposed too much, while liberals didn't think voting rights went far enough.

Kennedy had originally proposed the Civil Rights Act in the summer of 1963, and both he and Bobby had begun building working relationships with civil rights leaders like Martin Luther King Jr. And prior to his assassination, Kennedy was actively involved in recruiting Congressmen to support the bill. However, the legislation Kennedy supported would not resemble the one passed in 1964 by Lyndon Johnson; it was a limited civil rights act that focused primarily on voting rights but avoided more controversial topics like equal employment and desegregation. Kennedy, of course, had an eye on reelection and was aiming to toe the line between maintaining political support in the South while also holding liberal Democrats. His administration never gained any traction on a Civil Rights bill, with a coalition of Southern Democrats and Republicans preventing any action on one, and Kennedy knew that passage of the bill would be difficult. The legislation seemed certain to languish as Kennedy headed to Dallas with his eye on working toward his reelection.

Midterm Elections

The elections of 1962 represented a test of the popularity of the Kennedy Administration, and up to that point a series of crises had shaken the Kennedy White House. Other issues, including Civil Rights at home, had left many Americans unsure of the President.

The midterm elections that year were almost totally dominated by foreign policy. When political pundits talk about an "October Surprise," there could not be one more consequential or significant than the one that erupted with the Cuban Missile Crisis, which took place from October 16-28, ending just a week before the elections on November 6th. With the world bracing for nuclear war, the ballots cast on November 6th were definitely submitted with that crisis at the fore.

The results of the midterm elections were ultimately balanced. Unlike most midterms, the President's party did not shed seats in Congress. In the House of Representatives, the Democratic Party maintained resounding control of the chamber by losing just four seats. In the Senate, the results were equally tepid, with the Democratic majority increasing its hold on the body with three seats taken from Republicans.

As a litmus test, however, the midterm elections were certainly no reason for Kennedy to assume his reelection would be certain.

Reelection Prospects

By the fall of 1963, the Kennedy Administration was already gearing up for the following year's Presidential election. The election year was typically full of campaigning and politicking, necessitating a quick and early start.

Though looking back historically always involves many "what ifs," Kennedy's reelection prospects by 1963 were far from certain. His election in 1960 was one of the narrowest victories in history, and a small shift in just a handful of states could have tipped the balance towards the Republicans. There was no reason to think 1964 would necessarily be different.

Kennedy's domestic politics were cautious throughout his term in office. He toed the line on multiple fronts, hoping to maintain a steady hold on the Democratic South, while also maintaining control over the industrial Catholic states. But despite all of his efforts, this Democrats coalition was becoming increasingly tenuous, and the Civil Rights Movement increasingly threatened to tear it apart. The Southern faction and the Northern industrial faction were at odds over the issue of African-Americans for a second time in history, and it seemed the Party's national candidates would eventually need to choose to cater to one or the other. Kennedy consistently looked for ways to not have to make such a choice.

Still, his electoral prospects were hardly lost. Though he

personally seemed to attract little extra clout during his presidency, he had a built-in advantage: the Democratic Party itself. Since the days of Franklin Roosevelt, the Party had enjoyed control of Congress and the national government consistently, and there is little evidence that voters particularly disliked Kennedy by 1963. The 1962 elections did not overwhelmingly condemn Kennedy, and polling at the time suggested voters were generally positive about the President, just not overly enthusiastic.

The President was expected to enjoy another advantage in 1964, but one that remained uncertain. By 1964, the Republican Party had a long history of "me too-ism," the idea that the Democratic New Deal policies were so popular that the Republicans should not attempt to oppose them. Instead, the GOP had campaigned throughout the Eisenhower years on an acceptance of the New Deal, adding to it gradually and keeping its fundamentals intact. But a more conservative movement in the early part of the decade led by Arizona's Barry Goldwater threatened to undo Republican acceptance of the New Deal in order to replace it with a hardline conservatism not seen in American politics for over a generation. If Goldwater secured the Republican nomination, few pundits gave him a good chance against Kennedy, and he would indeed suffer a landslide defeat against Lyndon Johnson in 1964.

However, Goldwater's nomination to the Republican ticket was far from set in stone in 1963, and at the time it seemed Kennedy would likely face New York Governor Nelson Rockefeller, a much more moderate candidate who would be palatable to the electorate. There was no way of knowing Goldwater would get the nod in November 1963, and that month President Kennedy had to deal with the fact that he wasn't overly popular nationally. His foreign policy had a number of successes, but Americans had also not forgotten the failures of 1961 and early 1962. Furthermore, his tepid support of civil rights was dividing his own party, between liberals and conservatives. Southern conservatives thought Kennedy had proposed too much, while liberals didn't think voting rights went far enough. Sure enough, the strains would eventually undo the former Democratic coalition of the previous 80 years, done in with the help of Richard Nixon's "southern strategy" in the late 1960s, which saw the South turn solidly Republican at the expense of losing minority support. Lyndon Johnson privately predicted after the Civil Rights Act of 1964 that it ensured the Democrats had lost the South for a generation, and over 40 years later, the South continues to be Republican country in Presidential elections.

Planning a Trip to Texas

President Kennedy was already dealing with this political problem in 1963, and the division was already on display in the state of Texas, where sitting governor John

Connally was in conflict with his state's party over the issue. Connally was a former campaign manager for Lyndon Johnson's controversial 1948 Senate campaign, and as a conservative Democrat he was in conflict with liberal Democrats in the state over the issue of civil rights. The Party's division threatened to reduce President Kennedy's chances of carrying the state's absolutely vital 25 electoral votes in the 1964 election. John had made Lyndon Johnson his running mate over the objections of his brother Bobby in 1960 precisely for the purpose of winning Texas that year, which he barely did. It was clear how important Texas was to him, and as part of his reelection efforts the President decided to travel to the state to build support there nearly an entire year before the Presidential election.

Connally

Formally, the purpose of the trip to the Lone Star State in November 1963 was to sew up differences within the state's Democratic Party, but no one doubted that Kennedy hoped to win some votes along the way.

As it turned out, the Kennedy had vocalized the intent to make the fateful visit to Texas all the way back in 1962, and plans for the President's visit were put in place in June 1963 by Vice President Johnson and Texas Governor John Connally. The visit sought to deal with the state Democratic Party's conflict, which threatened to undermine the voter infrastructure necessary to turn out the votes for Kennedy in 1964. Governor John Connally and former opponent and sitting U.S. Senator Ralph Yaborough continued to have feuds over issues of race and economics in Texas, and Kennedy intended to smooth over these issues and reunite the party. Kennedy also hoped to jumpstart his campaign with some fundraising. By stopping in Houston, San Antonio, and Dallas, the President could meet with wealthy party regulars and collect some funds to begin the campaign.

Vice President Lyndon Johnson also had a substantial personal interest vested in the state. As a former U.S. Senator from Texas, Johnson was chosen for the Kennedy ticket in part to deliver the state. He managed that goal in 1960, but if he couldn't in 1964, it would be a significant embarrassment. With political ambitions of his own, being able to deliver it for Kennedy again was crucial, and for that reason Johnson would also be in Dallas on November 22, 1963.

Texas had always been a conservative state, and Kennedy was perceived as precisely the kind of Northeastern liberal Democrat that residents of the Lone Star State still don't favor politically, despite the fact the nation as a whole viewed the President as something of a moderate. Kennedy went to Texas knowing full well that many people there opposed his administration. When Kennedy's Ambassador to the United Nations, Adlai Stevenson, visited Dallas on October 24, 1963, he was met with jeers and was even hit by a sign and spat on. Dallas Police worried that Kennedy would receive similar treatment, and Stevenson personally warned the President about going to Dallas.

A handbill that circulated around Dallas on November 21, 1963 accusing President Kennedy of treason.

Just a few days before Stevenson's visit to Dallas, a young man named Lee Harvey Oswald had started working a seasonal job at the Texas School Book Depository.

Chapter 2: November 21, 1963

President Kennedy's trip to Texas began on November 21 with a flight from Washington to San Antonio, where he and Jackie arrived for what was supposed to be a two-day trip. Though he was well aware of the state's rough and tumble political culture, and he was aware of the attack on Adlai Stevenson less than a month earlier, Kennedy was undeterred. In fact, he relished the opportunity to leave Washington for a few days.

In San Antonio, President Kennedy, Vice President Johnson and Governor Connally dedicated the U.S. Air Force School for Aerospace Medicine. The school was a critical part of Kennedy's pledge to put a man on the Moon, so his attendance at the dedication was fitting. Later that day, Kennedy went off to Houston, where he spoke to a Latino-American organization and gave a speech honoring long-serving Congressman Albert Thomas at Rice University. Events like these were intended for public audiences, with political leaders not wanting to give the impression that the President had visited Texas merely to hobnob with important Democratic officials.

Kennedy ended November 21st in Fort Worth, where he slept for the evening. He was scheduled to speak to the area Chamber of Commerce the next morning at the Texas Hotel, and upon waking in the morning, Kennedy was asked to address a crowd that had gathered outside the

Texas Hotel. He opted to do so. Standing outside the hotel, despite the cold weather, Kennedy wooed the crowd, and the connection was palpable. Kennedy's off-the-cuff speech got rave reviews in the local press.

   After addressing the chamber on the national economy, Kennedy prepared to head to Dallas. He left from Carswell Air Field for what was only a 13 minute flight to Dallas aboard Air Force One. At approximately 11:40 a.m. CST, the President and First Lady were on the ground in Dallas. President Kennedy would be dead about an hour later.

Chapter 3: The Assassination of John F. Kennedy

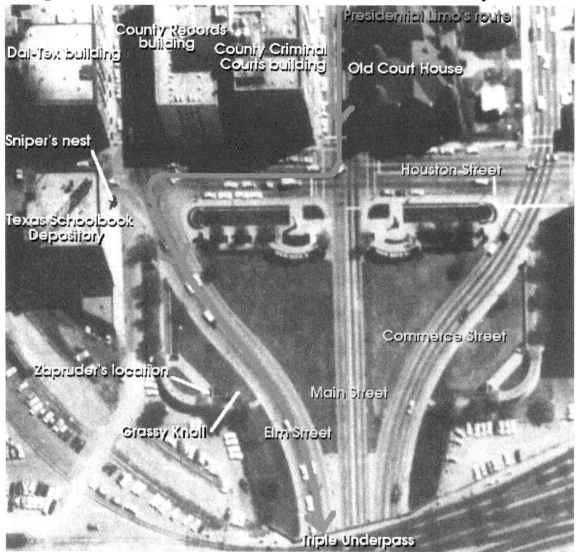

The motorcade route

Once they arrived in Love Field, President Kennedy and his wife greeted some well-wishers who had gathered to see the President disembark his plane, and Mrs Kennedy even received a bouquet of roses that she carried away with her. The First Couple were more than pleased with the warm reception they received, and Jackie opted to wear a bright pink Chanel suit for the occasion, a conspicuously fashionable choice even for her. Knowing full well that the country and press viewed her every fashion style with interest and fascination, Jackie fully intended to flatter with it.

The President was scheduled to speak at a luncheon at the Dallas Trade Mart, but with the fear that Kennedy's trip might be perceived as too private, the trip to the Trade Market was done to give him maximum public exposure. Thus, a public parade had been conceived for the President, and it was meant to be a lively affair. The President, First Lady, Vice President, Governor Connally and his wife would all drive through the streets of Dallas in this brief parade. Originally, the plan for the motorcade route was to simply stay straight on Main Street instead of turning onto Houston, but because Elm Street was the only way for the motorcade to reach the freeway from Dealey Plaza, the route was changed. Furthermore, if the motorcade stayed on Main Street, it would not offer as many people a chance to see the President publicly. Had the motorcade stayed on Main Street, it never would have been a target from the School Depository Building.

Leaving from Love Field, the President's motorcade consisted of seven vehicles. The first, a white convertible, contained the Dallas sheriff and some Secret Service agents. The second vehicle in the motorcade was the presidential limousine. In the presidential limousine, the Kennedys sat in the back seat, which was elevated a bit higher than the seats in front of them, where Governor

Connally and his wife were sitting. A driver and another Secret Service agent were also in the limousine. The third vehicle included aides and Secret Service agents, the fourth had the Vice President, Lady Bird Johnson and Senator Yarborough, and the fifth car had more agents. The last two cars were for members of the press.

At about 11:40 a.m., the President's motorcade departed Love Field, en route for the Trade Mart. The event was running about 10 minutes late due to the crowds that greeted the President at the airfield. Things had gone so well in his meetings with Democratic officials and in the reception they had received that President Kennedy chose to keep the Presidential limousine's top down, in order to feel more connected to the public that had lined the streets in anticipation of seeing the motorcade drive by. In fact, at two points on the route, the motorcade stopped so the President could shake hands with a group of nuns and schoolchildren.

Once the President's motorcade entered Main Street, it continued for a few moments before making a right turn onto Houston Street at about 12:29 p.m. As the motorcade turned onto Houston Street and entered Dealey Plaza, Governor Connally's wife turned around to Kennedy and said to him, "Mr. President, you can't say Dallas doesn't love you." Curiously, as the motorcade moved slowly down Houston Street, it was actually approaching a sniper's nest that had been set up on the sixth floor of the School Depository Building. Conspiracy theorists would later point out that the sniper's nest had a better view and thus an easier shot at the President as his motorcade slowly came toward the School Depository Building on Houston, thus making it inexplicable that a sniper from that position would wait for the motorcade to turn onto Elm Street and start moving away from the shooter.

Dealey Plaza, with the School Book Depository Building in the background and Elm Street in front of it.

Less than a minute later, it became clear that at least one person in Dallas did not love the President. As the motorcade made its way to Elm Street, it made a left turn onto Elm Street that brought the vehicles to a slow crawl. At approximately 12:30, as the motorcade started to slowly head down Elm Street, a number of shots rang out.

The view of Elm Street from the "sniper's nest" in the School Book Depository Building

Though there is still a heated debate over just how many shots were fired in Dealey Plaza that day, most witnessed claimed to have heard three, with the first coming shortly after the motorcade turned onto Elm Street. It is believed that the first shot missed, as evidenced by a study of the Zapruder film that seems to indicate members of the motorcade reacting to the sound of a shot before the President suffered any injuries. Most witnesses also claimed the first shot occurred as the President was waving.

If so, the second shot fired hit the President in the upper back and penetrated his throat before exiting his body around the knot of his tie. According to the Warren

Commission, this same bullet proceeded to strike Governor Conally in the armpit, crushing a rib and shattering his wrist upon exiting his body. Conspiracy theorists openly dismiss the notion that the same bullet wreaked such damage on both men and refer to it as the "Magic Bullet" theory, but a look at the Zapruder film shows Kennedy reacting to his injury and Connally reacting to his simultaneously.

At the time, Jackie initially thought there was a malfunction in the vehicle, not realizing what had happened until Governor Connally turned around and screamed. At that moment, Jackie created an indelible image by leaning in closer to her husband, whose hands had bunched up into fists as he was grasping at his neck. The concerned First Lady put her arm around the President, recognizing that he was wounded. At that moment, a second shot entered the rear of the President's head and shattered his skull, spraying blood, bone fragments and brain matter all over the vehicle's interior and on Mrs. Kennedy.

Jackie, in shock, then proceeded to start crawling along the back of the vehicle as Secret Service Agent Clint Hill, who had started running toward the limousine upon hearing shots fired, jumped onto the back and told her to get down in the seat. Hill later said he thought Mrs. Kennedy was reaching for a piece of the President's skull that had been blasted off in the attack. As the limousine quickly sped off underneath the underpass, Jackie reportedly told Mr. and Mrs. Connally, "They have killed my husband. I have his brains in my hand."

Over 100 witnesses in attendance that day would be interviewed, and though most believed that they heard the shots come from the vicinity of the School Book Depository Building, a strong percentage thought they heard shots fired from the grassy knoll that lined the Plaza. Some of the people were so sure that they scattered across the area in search of a sniper, though none was found. Others chose to lie down on the grass with their children as the shots were fired, afraid that more bullets were coming.

The grassy knoll

   With two grievously wounded men in the limousine, the President's motorcade predictably sped toward the nearest hospital, the University of Texas Parkland Hospital. Kennedy immediately entered a Trauma Room, where doctors began operating, but the emergency room doctors had realized from the beginning that his condition was "moribund", another way of saying he was dead on arrival. Regardless, they performed a traecheotomy and CPR, but to no avail. Meanwhile, the First Lady demanded to be let into the operating room, wanting to be with her husband when he died. Though she was initially denied, doctors relented and allowed her in. A priest was also called in to administer last rites. At 1:00 p.m. Central Standard Time, the President was declared dead. With that, Mrs. Kennedy put her wedding ring on her husband's finger and he was loaded into a casket. Governor Connally, meanwhile, was undergoing surgery for his wounds, and was not able to hear of the official news that the President had died.

Aside from the spectators who turned out to greet Kennedy and his wife at Dealey Plaza, some of the first to hear the news were those listening to Dallas radio. At 12:39, people listening to *The Rex Jones Show* were among the first to hear about the shooting: "This KLIF Bulletin from Dallas: Three shots reportedly were fired at the motorcade of President Kennedy today near the downtown section. KLIF News is checking out the report, we will have further reports, stay tuned." Television viewers who were watching a show on the local ABC affiliate found out around 12:45, when a news director who had been in Dealey Plaza ran back to deliver an impromptu news bulletin: Good afternoon, ladies and gentlemen. You'll excuse the fact that I am out of breath, but about 10 or 15 minutes ago a tragic thing from all indications at this point has happened in the city of Dallas. "Let me quote to you this, and I'll... you'll excuse me if I am out of breath. A bulletin, this is from the United Press from Dallas: 'President Kennedy and Governor John Connally have been cut down by assassins' bullets in downtown Dallas.'"

Outside of Dallas, the first people to find out about the shooting were those watching the soap opera *As the World Turns* on CBS. In the middle of the show, just minutes after Kennedy had been shot, Walter Cronkite cut in with a CBS News Bulletin announcing that President Kennedy had been shot at and was severely wounded: "Here is a bulletin from CBS News. In Dallas, Texas, three shots were fired at President Kennedy's motorcade in downtown Dallas. The first reports say that President Kennedy has been seriously wounded by this shooting. More details just arrived. These details about the same as previously: President Kennedy shot today just as his motorcade left downtown Dallas. Mrs. Kennedy jumped up and grabbed Mr. Kennedy, she called 'Oh, no!' The motorcade sped on. United Press says that the wounds for President Kennedy perhaps could be fatal. Repeating, a bulletin from CBS News, President Kennedy has been shot by a would-be assassin in Dallas, Texas. Stay tuned to CBS News for further details."

The news began to spread across offices and schools across the country, with teary-eyed teachers having to inform their schoolchildren of the shooting in Dallas. Most Americans left school and work early and headed home to watch the news. Even the normally stoic Cronkite couldn't hide his emotions. Acting Press Secretary Malcolm Kilduff had the unfortunate job of officially announcing the President's death to the world, which he did that day at 1:33 p.m. A few minutes later, around 1:40 p.m. CST, misty eyed and with his voice choked up, Cronkite delivered the news that the president was dead.

About a half hour later, the President's body, along with Vice President Johnson and Mrs. Kennedy, boarded Air Force One to return to Washington. With the President dead, Johnson was sworn in aboard Air Force One at around 2:38 p.m. that afternoon, with the former First Lady at his side in a blood-stained dress. Jackie continued to wear her pink outfit as an intentional reminder of what had just happened, and both she and the outfit were still full of the President's blood. Though she had washed her face and hair (something she later claimed she regretted), parts of John's skull were still on her.

The swearing-in was a first in many respects: never before had a President been sworn in to office in Texas, or by a woman. Judge Sarah Hughes was the most accessible judge in the area ready and able to swear-in the President. In his first official statement as president, Johnson told the shocked nation, "This is a sad time for all people. We have suffered a loss that cannot be weighed. For me, it is a deep, personal tragedy. I know the world shares the sorrow that Mrs. Kennedy and her family bear. I will do my best; that is all I can do. I ask for your help and God's."

Chapter 4: Chaos in Dallas

According to official investigations, about 90 seconds after shots were fired a young man named Lee Harvey Oswald was spotted by a policeman in the School Book Depository Building, but he did not seem out of breath and the police noticed no rifle or anything that would have made him seem suspicious. They let him pass after he was identified as an employee, and he allegedly exited the building around 12:33 p.m.

Just minutes later, at 12:40, Oswald boarded a city bus but quickly disembarked due to heavy traffic and took a cab home instead. He arrived there almost at precisely 1:00 p.m., just as President Kennedy's death was being pronounced.

Minutes before Oswald got home, a description of the potential shooter back in Dealey Plaza had been given to Dallas police. Howard Brennan, who had been sitting across the street from the School Book Depository Building, had already told police that he heard a shot come from above as the motorcade passed him, and when he looked up he saw a man with a rifle taking a shot from the corner window on the sixth floor of the building. He also claimed to have seen the same man looking out the same window a few minutes earlier. Brennan gave the best description he could, and it was already being broadcast to Dallas police officers within 15 minutes of the shooting. Around the same time, an employee at the Depository Building notified police that one of the men he supervised at the Building, Lee Harvey Oswald, was missing. Police would quickly find a high-powered rifle belonging to Oswald near the corner window of the sixth floor, with boxes arranged to create a "sniper's nest".

Oswald's housekeeper reported that Oswald briskly left

his home and began walking towards downtown. As he did so, a police officer named J.D. Tippitt pulled over to investigate Oswald around 1:15 p.m. Tippitt had been told by the owner of the Texas Book Depository that Oswald was the only man missing after the assassination. Tippitt, after pulling over, exited his car but was almost immediately shot and killed by Oswald.

Tippitt

A local shoe store owner saw the shooting and saw Oswald ducking in the alcove in his building. He later saw him enter a nearby theater without paying and notified the ticket booth at the theater, who notified police. Police arrived shortly after and confronted Oswald at 1:40 p.m. Oswald pulled a gun on the officer, but it misfired and he was arrested. As he was being taken away, he yelled loudly about police brutality.

Oswald being removed from the theater

As Oswald was brought into the police station for custody, reporters rattled him with questions. When asked if he killed the President, he said the question was the first time he'd heard of the President's death. He was also asked about his associations with the USSR. Investigations quickly unearthed the fact that Oswald had once been in the Marine Corps and was a proficient enough shooter that he was a sharpshooter during his time in the mid-'50s. He was also suspected of trying to assassinate retired U.S. Major General Edwin Walker presumably because of Walker's staunch anti-Communist views.

That day, stunned Americans wondered if the assassination was a Soviet conspiracy, a Cuban conspiracy, or the actions of a lone nut. Naturally, the interrogation of Oswald was dominated by those same concerns. Over the following days, police interrogated Oswald first about Tippitt's death and then the assassination of Kennedy. He could not keep his story straight when asked to account for himself at the time of President Kennedy's assassination. At one point, he said he was eating lunch, at another that he was working on the third floor. Amid conspiracies that Oswald was working for the Soviets, he was asked if he was a communist, to which he replied, "No, I am a Marxist." All throughout, Oswald insisted he was a "patsy", but investigators were certain he was lying. Oswald denied shooting Kennedy or Tippitt, even though his sniper rifle was found at the Depository and bullet casings at the scene of Tippitt's murder were traced back to the revolver found on Oswald when he was arrested in the theater. Oswald claimed two photographs of him holding both murder weapons were fakes, and he denied the statement by his co-worker that he had carried a long and heavy package to work on the morning of November 22.

On Sunday, November 24th, Oswald was being led through the Dallas jail's basement to be transferred to the county jail nearby, but a Dallas nightclub owner named Jack Ruby shot Oswald in the abdomen as he was being transferred. Oswald was taken to the same hospital where Kennedy was pronounced dead, where he was declared dead at 1:07 p.m. on November 24th, almost exactly 48 hours after the President was declared dead. Jack Ruby was quickly arrested, and right away the media began speculating that he had killed Oswald as part of a broader conspiracy.

Ruby approaches Oswald

Chapter 5: A State Funeral

After being flown back to Washington, Kennedy's body underwent an autopsy at the Bethesda Medical Center. Meanwhile, the Commanding General of the Military District of Washington began planning the President's state funeral. At Bethesda, the President's body was also prepared for burial.

President Kennedy's body was brought back to the White House, where it rested in repose in the East Room for 24 hours, draped in an American flag. Up to that time, Jacquie Kennedy had been with the body during each step of the voyage, but she agreed to leave it in the East Room alone so long as a Catholic priest was by its side. Two Roman Catholic priests were called in from the nearby Catholic University of America and prayed at the side of the body, while military guards stood in formation around it.   These hours in the East Room were for private viewings only.

The President's body in the East Room

The next day, the President's casket was taken in the same carriage that once carried Franklin Roosevelt's body to the Capitol. About 300,000 people came to Washington to watch the procession from the White House to the Capitol, which included a horse drawn carriage. There, he lay in state in the Capitol Rotunda, and over an 18-hour span, a public viewing flooded the Capitol with grieving citizens.

The viewing ended on Monday, November 25, at 9:30 a.m., with the President's funeral beginning promptly at 10:30. Because no funeral plans were drawn up prior to Kennedy's death, the precedent set by Abraham Lincoln's assassination was used as a model. Dignitaries from around the world and within the U.S. attended Kennedy's funeral, including all surviving presidents except Herbert

Hoover, who was too ill to attend (and died months later).

The President's body was brought from the Capitol to St. Matthew's Cathedral for a complete funeral. Throughout the funeral, brothers Ted and Bobby played important and visible roles in helping lead both the Kennedy family and the nation through the grieving process. They were with Jackie at all critical moments and helped organize and ensure that the state funeral went as smoothly as possible. The three of them had to visit the rotunda and escort the President's body out of the Capitol.

Mrs. Kennedy walked with both of her children as the procession moved to St. Matthew's. Famously, she instructed John Kennedy Jr. to salute his father's coffin as it passed. Sadly, his third birthday, November 25, 1963, coincided with the funeral. Deemed too young to attend the burial, the salute would be John Jr.'s final goodbye to his father.

After the funeral Mass, President Kennedy's body was taken to Arlington National Cemetery for burial. At the end of the burial service, approximately 3:34 p.m., Jackie lit the eternal flame that continues to burn above the

President's grave to this day. That famous tribute to Kennedy's memory was his wife's idea.

The internment of Kennedy at Arlington
President Kennedy's burial was the end of an era. Mrs. Kennedy and her children remained in the White House until December 5th, when they departed for a final time.

Chapter 6: Initial Investigations

Both the local Dallas Police Department and the FBI conducted early investigations of the Kennedy Assassination in its immediate aftermath. The Dallas Police were joined by the FBI and members of the Secret Service during the only interrogations of accused assassin Lee Harvey Oswald, who spoke little and never admitted to killing the President. A test was conducted to detect the presence of gunpowder on Oswald and turned up positive for his hands.

J. Edgar Hoover, director of the FBI, also conducted an investigation of the assassination in the immediate aftermath. Their investigation ended less than a month after the assassination and concluded that three bullets were fired: the first hit the President's shoulder, the second hit Governor Connally, and the third struck the President in the head, fatally wounding him. This would be contradicted in critical detail by the findings of the Warren Commission, and in 1979 the House Select Committee on Assassinations would declare in its findings that the FBI failed to adequately investigate whether Oswald's participation was part of a broader conspiracy.

In the days after the President's assassination, Americans across the country were on edge. Was this part of a broader conspiracy to sabotage the government? Were the Soviets involved and would this be a tactic they could employ repeatedly in the future? Lee Harvey Oswald's death only added a stronger shroud of uncertainty over the incident. He had, after all, claimed to be a Marxist before his own murder. Having died, however, the world would never know the truth of Lee Harvey Oswald, or if he was even the lone murderer.

Threats from within the country also surfaced as a topic of conversation. The rapid rise in power of both the CIA and the FBI in recent decades made many Americans suspicious of their role. Reportedly, two CIA agents were in Dallas at the time of the shooting. Why were they there? Were they involved or somehow complicit in the assassination of the President? Was American democracy unravelling at the seams?

While many of these questions were thrown off as outlandish and unsubstantiated, the conversation continued to broil, perturbing the American public. The death of John F. Kennedy was the first assassination in the modern era, with television and radio to announce it to the world in real time. Americans were rightly shocked.

Shortly after becoming President, Johnson hoped to end the conspiracies swirling around the Kennedy assassination by appointing the Warren Commission, a committee of prominent individuals charged with investigating the death of the President. Supreme Court Chief Justice Earl Warren was its chairman, thus the name "Warren Commission." Moreover, in the immediate aftermath of the assassination Johnson feared for his own life, believing the death could be part of a Soviet plot. He wanted concrete answers quickly.

The most famous and scrutinized investigation of the assassination started within a week, with the Warren Commission being established on November 29th, 1963. Along with Warren, the Commission consisted of seven very notable members of the American political community: Senator Richard Russell, a Georgia Democrat for whom a Senate Office Building is today named; Senator John Sherman Cooper, a Kentucky Republican; Representative Hale Boggs, the House Majority Leader; Representative Gerald Ford, the House Minority Leader and future U.S. President; CIA Director Allen Welsh Dulles; and John J. McCloy, former President of the World Bank. The group was diverse, wide-ranging and powerful.

The Warren Commission presenting its findings to President Johnson

The Commission spent an entire year trying to sort out the facts of the Kennedy assassination, and much of the investigation was conducted privately. As such, despite the fact its findings would be made public, there is little knowledge of the conversations that went on behind closed doors. A total of 94 testimonies took place with

Dallas residents and others who were present on the day of the assassination, and perhaps the most critical piece of evidence unearthed from the Warren Commission was the famous Zapruder Film. The film was shot near the grassy knoll in Dealey Plaza by a private citizen, Abraham Zapruder, and it caught the assassination on video, allowing the world to rewatch and investigate. Since he filmed from an elevated position, it has become the most memorable visual evidence, and it captured the fatal shot in excruciatingly grisly detail.

In the end, after a year of testimony, the Warren Commission issued its report to the President as the Warren Report on September 24, 1964. In it, the Warren Report contradicted some of the Dallas Police Department's earlier claims about the events of November 22, 1963. Warren agreed that three shots were fired, but they disagreed that all three hit either President Kennedy or Governor Connally. Instead, the Warren Report insisted that the second bullet hit Kennedy in the back, going through his throat to then strike Connally, and the third hit Kennedy in the head. The Warren Commission concluded the first bullet missed, contrary to the Dallas Police Report's investigation.

On other points, the Commission agreed with Dallas police and the FBI. For example, both thought there was only one gunman - likely Lee Harvey Oswald - and that he fired from the Texas Book Depository.

When the Warren Commission first commenced, many thought it might do more harm than good. While speculation about the Kennedy assassination was swirling, commentators thought a formal commission might be a lightning bolt for criticism, allowing for conspiracy theories to spread more widely. As it was, some of the findings were doubted by President Johnson, Bobby Kennedy, and even some of the Commission's members, all of whom expressed skepticism about certain points off the record.

As a result, a series of other lesser known investigations were conducted to try to discern the facts about the Kennedy assassination. The first of these came out of the White House and was known colloquially as the Rockefeller Commission. In 1975, President Gerald Ford had Vice President Nelson Rockefeller lead a commission called the United States President's Commission on CIA Activities within the United States. The purpose, as the name describes, was not entirely and exclusively to investigate Kennedy; instead, the Commission was charged with unraveling the full role of CIA operations within American borders.

With speculation about the role of the CIA in Kennedy's death swirling, however, the Commission could not avoid the topic. Specifically, the group looked at whether or not CIA operatives (and later Nixon henchman) E. Howard Hunt and Frank Sturgis were in Dallas on the day of the assassination and if they were involved. Some suggested that these men assassinated Kennedy and used Oswald as a cover up. Others thought Oswald was the assassin, but conspired with the CIA. The President's Commission, however, concluded that there was no substance to either of these claims and dismissed them.

The next committee to investigate the incident came out of the U.S. Senate. The Church Committee, known more formally as the United States Senate Select Committee to Study Governmental Operations with Respect to Intelligence Activities, was chaired by Senator Frank Church in 1975. Its express purpose was also not to investigate Kennedy but to survey the CIA and FBI in the wake of Watergate. The Commission hoped to better understand the role of the organizations in American life.

Unfortunately, the Church Committee came to a whole new conclusion: the FBI and CIA investigations of the Kennedy Assassination had been deficient and both organizations withheld valuable information from the Warren Commission. Gerald Ford, who was part of the Warren Commission, noted the CIA had kept certain evidence away from the Warren Commission because the Commission's investigation put "certain classified and potentially damaging operations in danger of being exposed." But naturally, conspiracy theorists, now completely unsure who to believe, began to think up more fanciful conspiracies than ever before.

Due to a whole new round of assassinations in the late 1960s, particularly the murders of Bobby Kennedy and Martin Luther King Jr., the House of Representatives decided to investigate assassinations for itself with yet another Committee. This time, the committee's purpose was explicit: assassinations. The United States House Select Committee on Assassinations took all that had been done and re-investigated it, opening new wounds again in 1976. Rather than putting conspiracy theories to rest, this new committee only lit the flames of existing theorists.

The Committee agreed with some findings of the Warren Commission but added others that were vague and left the doors open to wild ideas. First, the Committee agreed that Lee Harvey Oswald fired the fatal shot at the President and that he fired three times, hitting the President twice. However, their second conclusion was the one that proved most contested: the Commission agreed that it could not rule out the possibility of a second gunman on the grassy knoll. The House Committee believed that a Dictabelt audio recording of radio transmissions made by the Dallas Police Department Acoustic suggested that 4 shots were fired, not 3. Thus, the acoustic evidence left a "high probability" that a second gunman was present at the time of the shooting. The committee, however, was unable to identify a possible identity for the second gunman. Moreover, in subsequent years other scientists have refuted the acoustic evidence the House Committee relied on, claiming the Dictabelt recording of radio transmissions made by the Dallas Police Department did not dispositively indicate bullets were fired from elsewhere.

Among all its findings, one of the conclusions offered up by the House offered more fuel for the fire. It stated that the President's death was likely the result of a conspiracy, though it ruled out the participation of the Soviet Union, Cuba, or members of a government agency. The report went on to suggest that, while as a whole groups like organized crime and anti-Castro groups were not involved in Kennedy's death, individual members of these groups may have acted on their own.

Despite their controversial findings, the Commission apparently still sought to undermine conspiracy theories by stressing that the investigation it conducted took place over a decade after the shooting and was thus not able to access the best evidence possible.

Documentation of the Warren Commission and the various other commissions were highly valued in light of the conflicting reports of the assassination, but the processes and events surrounding the evidence of assassination only further inflamed conspiracy theorists. The original Warren Commission submitted its report to the National Archives in 1964, and general National Archives policy at the time stipulated that the documents be sealed for 75 years, which would have kept them under wraps until 2039.

Such lack of transparency, however, outraged Americans who wanted to know more about the assassination of their President. The Freedom of Information Act of 1966 changed the policy in an effort to offer more transparency of government operations to citizens. Unfortunately, not all documents relating to the Kennedy Assassination were immediately released at this time.

To get the documents fully released to the public, yet another commission was needed. This time, the Assassination Records Review Board was created out of the the President John F. Kennedy Assassination Records Collection Act of 1992. The Act sought to release all documents relating to Kennedy's death amid controversy and conspiracy theory. A recently-released movie, titled simply *JFK*, was part of the controversy then swirling around the assassination.

Still not all documents were released, though about 98% were made public over the next few years. The remaining documents, with very few exceptions, are to go public by 2017.

Chapter 7: Conspiracies

John F. Kennedy was assassinated nearly 5 decades ago, but today an overwhelming number of Americans do not believe the information conveyed by the Warren Commission. What they *do* believe is less certain, but the vast majority of Americans do not believe that Lee Harvey Oswald acted alone in the assassination of John F. Kennedy. Undoubtedly, the conflicting information given by the various government commissions played a role in this public perception.

Researchers sifted through the evidence and investigations used by the various commissions, and found significant holes. This added fodder to the fire of conspiracy theorists. The first obvious disturbing problem with the Kennedy investigation involved the death of numerous critical witnesses. This included, of course, Lee Harvey Oswald himself, the accused assassin, who was murdered by Ruby before a trial. While many Americans could accept that Oswald was the lone shooter, they are more apt not to believe that Oswald was a lone nut who was then shot 48 hours later seemingly at random by another lone nut. Ruby's murder of Oswald seemed too unbelievable to not be tied to a larger conspiracy.

Other prominent deaths included a woman named Dorothy Kilgallen, a prominent American journalist who studied politics and organized crime. Reportedly, she had interviewed Jack Ruby, Lee Harvey Oswald's assassin, when he was on trial for killing Oswald. While this information might have been incredibly useful in uncovering the relationships between the various characters surrounding the assassination, Dorothy Kilgallen died mysteriously on November 8th, 1965, from an overdose of alcohol and barbiturates. Unfortunately, medical examiners were unable to determine whether her death was simply an accidental overdose or a suicide. This other mysterious element – why she died so suddenly just hours after appearing on television – added another layer of mystery to the Kennedy death. Was she killed as part of a cover up?

Even Jack Ruby's death came relatively early, of lung cancer in 1967. Considering his death came shortly after the President's, many suspected that he knew of his lung cancer in 1963, and that it motivated him to become involved in a cover up, knowing he would die before information could be divulged.

Other deaths in the Kennedy conspiracy included numerous Mafia members before 1970. This included as many as 10 people. Additionally, more people related to Jack Ruby died, incuding four of the showgirls who worked at his club. All of these deaths coming in a relatively short time span, related to organized crime or the figures known to be involved with the assassination, only hardened the views of conspiracy theorists.

The final major committee investigating Kennedy's death in the House opened a huge door for conspiracy theories by legitimizing the idea of multiple gunmen. To be an authentic "conspiracy," more than one person needed to be involved, so conspiracy theorists jumped on this evidence.

The Warren Commission concluded that the three shots fired at the President's motorcade took place within a 4.8 to 7 second timeframe, and most witnesses agreed that the shots were not evenly spaced out, with a noticeable delay between the first and second shots and a much smaller amount of time between the second and third shots. Given that Oswald was a former Marine with plenty of experience firing his own gun, people can accept that he could fire three shots in such a tight time frame, but if the acoustic evidence correctly suggested 4 shots were fired, it would have been impossible for the sniper in the School Book Depository Building to fire them all in 7 seconds. Furthermore, it's unclear why Oswald, who knew what he was doing with a high-powered rifle, would space out his shots unevenly. On top of that, Governor Connally himself suggested to the Warren Commission that, as the motorcade was being fired at, he thought more than one gunmen was firing. He reportedly told his wife "they're going to kill all of us!" as bullets were flying.

Of course, there were also plenty of witnesses on the ground – spectators eager to see the President – had a different view of the assassination than the Warren Commission. Many in attendance at the time of the assassination thought the shots were fired from the famous grassy knoll along the President's route. The Warren Commission, on the other hand, discounted this theory, believing the bullets all came from the Texas

Book Depository. Others believed that at least one shot came from the Dal-Tex Building, which was immediately across from the Texas Book Depository. Employees in that building reported that the shots they heard were loud enough to have been from their building.

Other evidence overlooked by the Warren Commission corresponds with a theory of multiple gunmen. The only spectator injured in the assassination, James Tague, was injured on his right cheek when a bullet ricocheted towards him. According to researchers, however, the trajectory of the bullet that struck Tague was not consistent with one fired from the Texas Book Depository.

All of these conflicted reports, when taken together, lead conspiracy theorists to believe that more than one gunman fired the shots that killed President Kennedy. How else could so many different people believe fundamentally different things about the events of November 22, 1963?

Aside from the belief that Oswald wasn't the only shooter, conspiracy theories have focused on several suspects. One major conspiracy theory suspect was a straightforward one: Lyndon Johnson, who notoriously did not get on well with Bobby Kennedy and felt isolated and powerless as John's Vice President. The theory is that he wanted the President dead so that he could occupy the White House.

The first time this idea gained major traction came in

1968 with a book titled *The Dark Side of Lyndon Baines Johnson.* The book posited that Lyndon Johnson led a ring of Dallas-area FBI members, CIA agents and police officials who conspired to assassinate the President. Johnson was from Texas, the site of Kennedy's death, so the book thought the site was fitting for the Johnson-motivated assassination.

In 2003, the Johnson debate reignited with a book titled *Blood, Money and Power.* This book gave a more elaborate explanation of Johnson's involvement. According to the book, he conspired with a Dallas-area lawyer friend and that the two worked out the placement of an associate on the 6th floor of the Texas Book Depository who later shot the President. Oil magnates paid the assassin, and they were rewarded with oil-positive legislation during Johnson's term.

Madeline Brown, who claimed to be Johnson's mistress, later said that she had firsthand knowledge of Johnson's involvement in Kennedy's assassination. Other figures also intervened to add fodder to the Johnson Conspiracy. Lee Harvey Oswald's surgeon at the Parkland Hospital reportedly spoke to Johnson on the phone as Oswald was entering the hospital. According to him, Johnson demanded a death-bed confession from Oswald, stating he killed the President. This, conspiracy theorists believe, indicated that Johnson wanted someone to cover up the assassination and silence any speculation about Johnson.

Most credible historians refute the Johnson conspiracy. On the contrary, many professional historians note Johnson had his own conspiracy theory; he thought the murder was the fault of Castro's Cuba. Despite these private beliefs, however, he tried to keep his beliefs quiet out of fear that making them public might ignite a Soviet-American nuclear war over the fate of Cuba.

The CIA and the FBI are together taken as the most suspicious government entities potentially involved with the Kennedy Assassination. Conspiracy theorists point to numerous pieces of evidence to implicate them.

The first major piece surrounds Lee Harvey Oswald's relationship to government agency. In the past, he had received suspicious preferential treatment that suggests something questionable. Oswald, an avowed communist, had previously moved to the Soviet Union but was allowed to repatriate to the United States after speaking with officials from the State Department. Such a move to the USSR and back to the U.S. was rare; at the time, Americans leaving for the USSR were viewed with extreme suspicion and were rarely allowed to return. Oswald, on the other hand, was allowed to return with an almost $500 repatriation loan to boot.

Other pieces of evidence allegedly chronicle a deep Oswald-CIA relationship. Just a week before the assassination, Oswald reportedly showed up at the Dallas FBI office and asked to speak with agent James Hosty.

The Warren Commission knew of this relationship, but when it asked for letters of correspondence between Hosty and Oswald, Hosty had all of them destroyed by orders from his superiors. For this, Hosty was reprimanded and transferred to an office in Kansas City. Those who dismiss these conspiracy theories suggest that Oswald actually left a letter threatening to attack or bomb the FBI office.

Oswald had other relationships with the CIA and FBI. After being arrested in New Orleans in August of 1963, he asked to speak with an FBI agent and did so, which conspiracy theorists allege is highly unusual for someone arrested on a charge of disturbing the peace. He spoke for over an hour to Agent John Quigley.

Many who knew Oswald or were involved with the CIA thought Lee Harvey Oswald was an employee for the Agency. Members of the Tokyo CIA Office leaked to the press that Oswald had been sent to Russia as a spy in the 1950's. Even Oswald's mother stated that Oswald was sent to Russia "by the government" in 1959.

With this evidence, conspiracies diverge. Some suspect Oswald was hired by the CIA to kill the President. Others thought Oswald was not the assassin, but that the CIA used him as a scapegoat after he began to dissent from CIA activities.

Perhaps the most widely believed conspiracy theory, and certainly the least radical, is that President Kennedy was assassinated as part of a mob conspiracy. Those who believe this theory point to the fact that Attorney General Bobby Kennedy had been a thorn in the side of organized crime for over a decade, including during his brother's administration. It's also widely assumed that Jack Ruby, as a notorious Dallas nightclub owner, was in a line of business that would have possibly connected him to the criminal underworld. To conspiracy theorists, mob ties explain Ruby's actions better than the notion that he simply snapped and decided to try to kill Oswald in revenge for his assassination of the President.

Chapter 8: Legacy

Lincoln and Kennedy

As Americans tried to make sense of Kennedy's life and death, the mythology enveloping his presidency popped up quickly. Aside from the label of his presidency as Camelot, people looked to the links between Kennedy and another beloved assassinated President: Abraham Lincoln. One of the first major fascinations surrounding Kennedy's assassination focused on the seeming coincidences between the assassinations of John F. Kennedy and Abraham Lincoln. These have since become well known among Americans, even if they are full of exaggerations and easy to explain coincidences.

The first similarity between the two involved their political history. Lincoln was elected to Congress in 1846, Kennedy in 1946. Both men were runners-up for their party's Vice Presidential nomination in 1856 and 1956 respectively. Lincoln was elected President in 1860, Kennedy in 1960. As President, both had Vice Presidents with the last name Johnson: Lincoln had Andrew Johnson, Kennedy has Lyndon Johnson.

Other minor things surround the two men. Lincoln's Vice President was born in 1808, Kennedy's in 1908. Both suffered the death of a child in the White House, a rare occurrence in American history. Some people even point to the most basic coincidence, like the fact both Presidents also had seven letters in their last names.

Regarding their assassinations, the similarities are also noteworthy. Both Presidents were assassinated by men whose full names consisted of 15 letters and who are known by their full names (although this is not unique among assassins, as in the case of John Lennon's killer, Mark David Chapman): John Wilkes Booth and Lee Harvey Oswald. Both Presidents were assassinated on a Friday by being shot in the back of the head in the presence of their wives.

Lincoln was shot in Ford's Theater, while Kennedy was shot in a Lincoln vehicle made by Ford Auto, and both assassins were killed before they could be tried. Worse, both men sympathized with an organization or body that was an enemy of the United States: in Booth's case, it was the Confederate States of America, in Oswald's, the Soviet Union.

And of course, Kennedy's coffin rested on the Lincoln Catafalque, which was originally used for Lincoln's coffin in 1865 and is still used for state funerals.

Lincoln Catafalque

These mysterious coincidences began appearing in the mainstream public as early as 1964. The American people, already unsure what to make of the Kennedy assassination, had found yet another aspect of Kennedy's life and death to envelop in mystery, intrigue, and mythology.

Remembering November 22, 1963

November 22nd, 1963, much like September 11th, 2001,

and December 7th, 1941, is a date that any American old enough to have lived through it remembers vividly. Just about anyone above the age of 5 can remember where they were and what they were doing when they learned of the first assassination of a President in the modern era. Unlike previous assassinations – the most recent being William McKinley's in 1901 – Kennedy's was broadcast live over radio and television. Television reporters teared up as they delivered the news. And unlike other Presidents, whose faces were pasted in newspapers with no voice or sound, Kennedy was a well-known celebrity. His presidency was the first to be dominated by multiple forms of real-time media, making his death feel that much more intimate and tragic to Americans.

Furthermore, the fact that Kennedy's assassination practically played out in real time, with only minutes separating the assassination and news reports about it, has likely contributed to the conspiracy theories surrounding his death. Unlike other assassinations, Americans were able to study and reflect on the events for themselves rather than read a predetermined story in their local newspaper. By delivering the assassination via radio and television in real time, reporters did not have all the facts, giving the American people the impression that much was unknown and that a conspiracy or cover-up was possible.

Other social factors contribute to the mystery of John F. Kennedy's assassination. In an era when the American government was becoming more powerful and invasive than ever before, Americans were increasingly skeptical of entities like the CIA and FBI. They became good scapegoats for the greatest American tragedy since World War II.

In the end, Americans are left to decide for themselves who killed John F. Kennedy. With many of the prominent players now gone and the evidence slim, perhaps the country will never know how exactly its President died. Either way, the event served as a significant moment in the history of the United States, and it has come to symbolize the turbulent transition from the tranquil '50s to the troublesome '60s.

Online Resources

Other titles about 19th century history by Charles River Editors

Other titles about 20th century history by Charles River Editors

Other titles about presidential assassinations on Amazon

Bibliography

Deeb, Michael J. *The Lincoln Assassination: Who Helped John Wilkes Booth Murder Lincoln?*

Iuniverse.com: 2011.

O'Reilly, Bill. *Killing Lincoln: The Shocking Assassination that Changed America Forever.*

New York: Henry Holt, 2011.

Schwartz, Barry. *Abraham Lincoln and the Forge of National Memory.* Chicago: University of

Chicago Press, 2000.

Johns, A. Wesley (1970). The Man Who Shot McKinley. South Brunswick, New Jersey: A.S. Barnes.

Leech, Margaret (1959). In the Days of McKinley. New York: Harper and Brothers.

Miller, Scott (2011). The President and the Assassin. New York: Random House.

Olcott, Charles (1916). William McKinley 2. Boston: Houghton Mifflin. Retrieved March 23, 2012.

Rauchway, Eric (2004). Murdering McKinley: The Making of Theodore Roosevelt's America. New York: Hill and Wang.

Ackerman, Kenneth D. (2003). Dark Horse: The Surprise Election and Political Murder of President James A. Garfield. New York: Carroll & Graf Publishers.

Hayes, Henry Gillespie; Hayes, Charles Joseph (1882). A Complete History of the Life and Trial of Charles Julius

Guiteau, Assassin of President Garfield. Philadelphia: Hubbard Brothers.

Rosenberg, Charles E. (1968). The Trial of the Assassin Guiteau: Psychiatry and the Law in the Gilded Age. Chicago: University of Chicago Press.

Peskin, Allan (1978). Garfield: A Biography. Kent, Ohio: Kent State University Press.

Free Books by Charles River Editors

We have brand new titles available for free most days of the week. To see which of our titles are currently free, click on this link.

Discounted Books by Charles River Editors

We have titles at a discount price of just 99 cents everyday. To see which of our titles are currently 99 cents, click on this link.

CPSIA information can be obtained
at www.ICGtesting.com
Printed in the USA
LVHW062349300522
720044LV00034B/1389